AMAZING BUT TRUE

SPORTS

STORIES

STEVE RIACH

GIFT BOOKS
from Hallmark

Amazing But True Sports Stories
by Steve Riach

Copyright © 2004
Hallmark Licensing, Inc.
ISBN: 1-59530-036-8

Published by Hallmark Books,
a division of Hallmark Cards, Inc.,
Kansas City, MO 64141

Visit us on the Web at *www.Hallmark.com*.

Printed in the USA

BOK2042

ABOUT THE AUTHOR

S teve Riach is president and co-founder of VisionQuest Communications Group, Inc., a Dallas-based media company. He is an award-winning producer, writer, and director of many television, film, and video projects, and is one of the nation's foremost creators of positive-themed sports content. Steve's programs have been featured on ESPN, FOX Sports, NBC, PAX-TV, and a variety of other outlets.

Steve has authored several books, including *Passion for the Game, Above the Rim, The Drive to Win, Inspire a Dream, It's How You Play the Game, Life Lessons from Auto Racing, Life Lessons from Golf, Life Lessons from Baseball,* and *Heart of a Champion: Profiles in Character.*

He is also co-founder of the *Heart of a Champion Foundation,* a non-profit organization devoted to teaching character and virtue to children. Steve is creator and author of the foundation's *Heart of a Champion Character Development Program,* which is used in schools across the country. (To learn more about the foundation, visit the Web site at www.heartofachampion.org, or call (972) 690-4588.)

A former college baseball player at the University of the Pacific, Steve is also a sought-after speaker to school groups, youth agencies, corporations, sports organizations, and churches.

ACKNOWLEDGEMENTS

A *mazing But True Sports Stories* is the result of years of research and documentation. As with projects of this magnitude, I received much help from many caring people. I would like to thank the following:

My wife, Wendy, and children, Kristen, Josh, and Elissa, who have unselfishly given me their constant love and support and allowed me the necessary quiet time to write.

My crack research aide for this book, Nelson Staats, who did a wonderful job in the many hours he spent researching stories, gathering information, and chasing down leads at all hours.

My good friends Dr. Lance Rawlings and Brad Thomas, who initially shared a few of these stories with me, and were always available to chuckle about the rest of them.

John Humphrey, my business partner at VisionQuest, who helped conceive and develop this book.

Harold Reynolds, James Brown, and Clark Kellogg, who, during the course of my relationship with them, inspired concepts for a book such as this.

Joe Gibbs, Nolan Ryan, Pat Summerall, Larry Nelson, and Darrell Waltrip, some of the finest men in all of sports, who, through involvement in my previous books, have demonstrated their desire to have a positive influence on our culture.

The Board of Directors of the Heart of a Champion Foundation, for their commitment to seeing sports stories used to help shape character in young people across America.

And, finally, Todd Hafer at Hallmark, who has been the driving force behind this book coming about and has been a true joy to work with.

Thank you all!

THE PENCIL IS MIGHTIER THAN THE PUTTER

It is one of the most renowned blunders in all of sport, and it happened on one of sport's biggest stages. With a national audience following closely, Roberto de Vicenzo was on the verge of winning the 1968 Masters Tournament, when he snatched defeat from the jaws of victory, through the power of his pencil.

Mr. de Vicenzo birdied the 17th hole at Sunday's final round at Augusta, and the crowd gathered around the 17th green began to cheer wildly. They the broke into a rousing rendition of "Happy Birthday," helping de Vicenzo celebrate his birthday.

Perhaps it was that distraction that caused de Vicenzo to suffer a momentary memory lapse and mark down a 4 rather than a 3 on his scorecard. Or, perhaps it was the nervousness he felt as he realized how close he was to winning golf's greatest prize—the green jacket. Regardless, when the tip of his pencil completed tracing the 4, de Vicenzo was finished.

At the end of the round, de Vicenzo and Bob Goalby appeared to be tied for the lead and headed for a playoff round the following day. However, when the scorecards were totaled, de Vicenzo score totaled 278, one stroke more than Goalby's 277. It was then that de Vicenzo realized his error at the 17th hole. But under PGA rules, no alteration is allowed on a scorecard after a player has signed it.

Since de Vicenzo had already signed and turned in his scorecard, the tournament had no choice but to uphold the rules. Goalby became the Masters champion, and de Vicenzo was left with a bad birthday memory.

JOEL EDWARDS:
Playing the Fair Way

For 12 years, Joel Edwards had been grinding it out on the PGA tour, trying to pick up his first victory. He had been teased with a number of close finishes. He had come back from serious injury. He had lost and regained his tour playing card. Along the way he carried the pressure of providing for his family.

But when Edwards stepped on the course for the 2001 The Players Championship, he was feeling good about his chances in what would be his biggest tournament of the year. He had tied for fifth in his previous tournament and seemed to be putting things together.

On the very first hole of Thursday's first round, Edwards narrowly missed a putt for par. The ball lay but three inches from the cup. As he was getting ready to tap the ball in, just before his putter impacted the ball, Edwards noticed the ball move ever so slightly. He followed through with his stroke and the ball rattled into the cup. It was a first hole bogey and a start to a score of even-par 72 in round one. The first day was over, and Edwards was not in bad position as he prepared for the next day and round two.

But something didn't feel right. Edwards kept thinking about that putt on hole number one. Throughout the afternoon, as he hit balls on the driving range, talked with other players, and ate dinner, that putt consumed his thoughts. He replayed the image over and over in his mind and asked himself the questions: Was the ball rolling? Had he broken a rule by hitting a moving ball?

"When it first happened, I knew there was a rule or something, but I didn't lose a ball or anything like that so I just blew it off," Edwards said. "The ball turned maybe a millimeter. I said, 'Dadgum, I've already signed my scorecard and I'm going well. I don't think it's that big a deal.'"

Edwards played on, shooting well enough on Friday to advance to the weekend rounds. But on Saturday, just after he had hit a shot near the pin on the 13th hole, he decided he couldn't go on any longer without doing something about the moving ball. He had no idea if he had broken a rule, but the fact that he couldn't get it out of his mind convinced him he needed to discuss it with an official. Following the round, he went straight to the tournament director and told him of the situation. Officials asked him if he had touched the ground with the putter prior to hitting the ball. Edwards said he didn't remember, but that 9 times out of 10 he usually did, so he must have. The officials said they wouldn't penalize Edwards unless he could say his club touched the ground. So Edwards disqualified himself on the spot, shook hands with the officials and walked away. With his head held high. "I'd rather live with an honest mistake and admit it than live for the rest of my life knowing I made last-place money and it may have been tainted in a way," Edwards said. "It was not worth feeling like this.

"My dad was one of those people who said, 'Son you've got to stand for who you are, and if you don't do that then you're being dishonest with yourself.' And if you're honest with yourself, you can go on and be the person you want to be."

Integrity won out in the end, and Joel Edwards penalized himself even though he was unsure he had actually violated a rule.

"These rules and this sport are pure," Edwards said. "I want to know that what I earned is what I earned. This game doesn't owe anybody anything. You're blessed to be able to play it."

SO YOU WANT TO BE A REFEREE?

Veteran basketball officials Cliff Ogden and Alex George learned first-hand just how difficult a referee's job can be. The year was 1956, and Ogden and George were officiating a game between the University of Wichita and the University of Detroit, played on Wichita's home court—which was known in those days for hosting crowds that were unruly and often inebriated.

Detroit was down by one point with four seconds to play as they began to inbound the ball. They pushed the ball into the frontcourt and, before time ran out, a Detroit player was able to get off a shot. As Ogden and George both followed the arc of the ball toward the hoop, they were shocked to see that a Wichita fan had tossed an overcoat from the field house balcony and landed it right over the rim. The ball hit the coat and bounced off as the buzzer sounded.

Ogden and George were faced with a situation they had never encountered

before. As they contemplated
what call to make, they were
surrounded by a wild mob of
Wichita fans who were scrambling
across the court, celebrating.

George turned to Ogden and
said, "It's a hundred and twenty feet to
our dressing room, and I'm not going
to call anything until we both get to
the door."

With the door locked behind
the two officials, George notified
both teams that he had called
the shot good, and the basket
gave Detroit a one-point win.

Wisely, Ogden and George waited
until they could hear no fans remaining in
the Wichita field house before leaving their dressing room and
heading home.

It was a situation they hoped they would never face again.

ALL STAR-SPANGLED TEAM:

G WORLD B. FREE
G CLAUDE ENGLISH
C GEORGE WASHINGTON
F MARCUS LIBERTY
F KEITH STARR

ALL THE PRESIDENT'S MEN:

G NORM NIXON
G EARL MONROE
C GEORGE WASHINGTON
F GENE KENNEDY
F GARFIELD HEARD
G TJ FORD
G GARY GRANT
C ROOSEVELT BOWIE
F VINCE CARTER
F RICHARD JEFFERSON

TAKING THE FIFTH

Football referees are rarely considered generous. But during a tight college football game, one popular ref was accidentally more accommodating than he would have liked.

Red Friesell was one of the most respected referees in college football. So it came as a surprise when he became the center of controversy during a game between Cornell and Dartmouth on November 18, 1940. The field was slick and muddy from late-fall rains that hit Hanover, New Hampshire, Dartmouth's home. Cornell, an Eastern football power at the time, was on the short end of a 3-0 score. It looked as though they were about to be upset as the clock wound down. But then the Big Red mounted one last strong drive, moving down the field all the way to the Dartmouth 6-yard line. There, the Mean Green defense prepared for one last stand. Cornell ran three consecutive running plays to move the ball to the 1-yard line. The Big Red was then penalized for attempting to call a time-out when they did not have one. Friesell moved the ball back to the 6.

On fourth down, Cornell attempted a pass, which fell incomplete. But after retrieving the ball, Friesell reset the line of scrimmage at the 6-yard line once again. No one noticed Cornell had already run out of downs, so the two teams lined up for play, with Cornell still on offense. After the snap, Cornell again attempted a pass, and this one was completed

for a "fifth-down" touchdown on the game's final play. The Red won the game 7-3.

Amid the excitement at the finish, Friesell's error went unnoticed. However, shortly after the game ended, players, press, and fans all agreed that Cornell had been given an extra down and the winning points should not count.

Friesell was disheartened after the game, telling the press that he "blew it." In his official report, he accepted responsibility for the error, and absolved the other three officials from any blame.

Cornell's response was equally demonstrative of their character. They returned the victory to Dartmouth, which ended the Red's 18-game winning streak.

Ivy League Commissioner Asa Bushnell put the finishing touches on one of the most amazing finishes to a college football game, when in a telegram to Friesell, he mused, "Don't let it get you down, down, down, down, down."

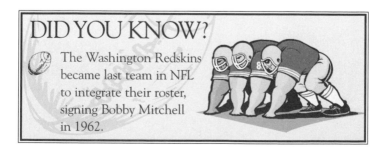

DID YOU KNOW?

The Washington Redskins became last team in NFL to integrate their roster, signing Bobby Mitchell in 1962.

BASEBALL'S ALL-ROMANCE TEAM:

ELLIS VALENTINE

CUPID CHILDS

SANDY AMOROS

BOBBY VALENTINE

PETE ROSE

JIM RAY HART

STEVE SPARKS RON DARLING RICH BATCHELOR

PAUL CASANOVA

RICK SWEET

Util. **JIMMY RING**

LITTLE BEGINNINGS

I magine a great sports career that almost ended on the day it began.

Randy Johnson is a baseball superstar, an intimidating 6'10" left-hander who has been one of the most dominant pitchers of his time. A fireballer who has been feared by hitters throughout the game, Johnson is among baseball's all-time strikeout leaders, and has been honored with the Cy Young Award in both the American League, as a member of the Seattle Mariners, and in the National League, as a member of the world-champion Arizona Diamondbacks. But Johnson's historic career almost never got started.

Johnson vividly recalls his first experience with organized baseball. He was six years old and decided to attend a Little League tryout in his hometown of Livermore, California, about 25 miles east of Oakland.

"I went there by myself because my mom and dad both worked," he recalls. "There I was with a bunch of other kids, feeling like a lost puppy dog. I didn't know where to go, who to see. I got lost, started crying, and went home."

Johnson's mother soon arrived home and found her young son sitting inside the house, crying. When she learned of Randy's experience and his fears, she decided to march him right back out to the tryout. So she took Randy by the hand, walked back to baseball fields, convinced her son to participate in the tryouts, and had him placed on a Little League team. The rest is truly history.

"She knew I wanted to play," Johnson says. "And when I think about it, if she hadn't taken me back, I might not be where I am today."

DID YOU KNOW?

Hack Wilson is the shortest home-run champ in Major League history, at 5'6."

BASEBALL'S ALL-HOME BUILDERS TEAM

Major League Baseball Lineup Card

Team	HOME BUILDERS	Date
Pos.	Player	Substitution
C	PHIL ROOF	
1B	MICKEY MANTLE	
2B	JAY BELL	
SS	ANDY SHEETS	
3B	JIM DAVENPORT	
OF	MATT STAIRS	
OF	ROWLAND OFFICE	
OF	DON LOCK	
OF	TERRY PUHL	
P	JIMMY KEY	
P	DENNIS LAMP	
P	JOHN ROCKER	
P	TOM HOUSE	
P	STAN WALL	
P	DICK POLE	

OFF THE TEE
AND UP A TREE

E very golfer has his or her share of
humorous or embarrassing moments
while going for the prize in the heat of a
tournament. As everyone who has ever hit
that little round ball with any club from the
bag knows, once the ball is struck, anything
can happen. With a strange bounce, a wild
kick off of an object, or an unusual roll, the ball can wind up
anywhere. Even in a tree.

While most duffers would think such things happen only
to them, even the golf's top players have similar experiences.

Such was the case for two-time Masters champion
Bernhard Langer early in his career. "There have been many
times when crazy things have happened," he remembers.

Two of Langer's funniest memories have made golf's
version of blooper reels. The first instance took place at a
tournament in England in 1980. In this particular instance,
Langer needed three swings of the club to hit the ball 20 yards.

"I had two air shots," Langer recalls. "I was, like, twenty
yards from the green in some heather in England. It's thick
rough. I walked in there and thought, 'Oh, it's going to be a
terrible lie.' I go there [to the ball], and it's sitting right on top
of this grass about a foot high. I hit right under the ball—I
went under it, and the ball went down."

Langer's pitching wedge became an instant weed-whacker,

but rather than hit the ball, he merely trimmed the heather. So, he tried again. Once again, more heather trimming, but no ball striking.

He says, "I hit it again and it went down. And I said to myself, 'I can't believe this. You're twenty yards away [from the hole], and you can't hit the ball.' So, the third time, I finally hit it and got it out of there. I just shook my head and said, 'You know, this is golf.'"

There were plenty of others shaking their heads when Langer had a second strange experience. Once again, for a moment, he was more landscaper than golfer, and he came away not only with a memory, but also a new nickname.

It happened during another tournament in England, this one in 1982. This time, Langer found himself up a tree—literally.

"I was playing the 17th hole when I pulled my second shot, a nine iron, to the left. I heard the ball hit a big oak tree near the green two or three times, but never saw it come down," Langer recalls. "As I approached the green I could hear the spectators laughing. Sure enough, the ball was lodged up in the tree about fifteen feet above the ground in a little indentation on a huge branch. I debated whether I should take the penalty shot or climb up in the tree and hit it."

What would any competitive elite professional golfer do?

"I climbed up the tree and hit it out of there and onto the green," Langer says.

Playing months later in the United States, Langer realized that word of the incident had followed him across the Atlantic Ocean.

"I heard a couple in the crowd talking about me," he remembers. "'There's the guy who was in the tree,' one spectator said. 'What's his name?' The other replied, 'I think it's Bernhard something.' 'No, it's not,' said the other. 'That's Tarzan!'"

"I wasn't too amused at the time. But when you look back, it's quite funny."

BAT BOY

Although Rex Hudler played only a handful of games with Cal Ripken Jr. in the Baltimore Orioles' infield, the two developed a strong friendship over their years in baseball.

"We played against each other in the minor leagues, but I really got to know him when I was in the Orioles organization in nineteen eighty-six and eighty-seven," recalls Hudler.

By the time they played together in Baltimore, it was clear who was the better player. Ripken was baseball's all-time iron man, and Hudler was toiling for the second of a half-dozen Major League teams he wound up playing for, not counting a stint in Japan. However, when the players came out of high school, few scouts had Ripken pegged as the better big-league prospect of the two.

"Cal and I were drafted the same year— seventy-eight," Hudler explains. "And I never let him forget I was drafted ahead of him."

Hudler was a first-round draft choice of the New York Yankees in 1978; Ripken was a selected by the Baltimore Orioles in the second round. By 2001, both had retired from the game; Ripken as one of the greatest players in the history of the game; Hudler as one of the game's memorable personalities—a journeyman utility player who was a hustling, encouraging, chatter-box of energy.

Eight years after they entered professional baseball at the same time, the two men finally had a chance to play together and begin a friendship. They played next to each other during the '86 and '87 seasons, Ripken at his usual shortstop position, and Hudler at 2nd base. While Hudler learned much about the game from baseball's all-time iron man, it was off the field where Ripken gave Hudler his biggest tip.

During spring training in Florida before the 1987 season, Ripken coached Hudler on the proper way to propose to his wife-to-be, Jennifer Myers.

"Rex couldn't figure out how to ask me," Jennifer recalls. "It's one of the few times I've ever seen him at a loss for words."

So, Ripken gave the nervous rookie a big-league idea—charter a sailboat out of Key Biscayne, and wait until sunset to

DID YOU KNOW?

 Former catcher Moe Berg was a spy during WWII.

 Joe Torre is the first manager to lose 1,000 games before winning 1,000.

 The 1962 New York Mets had teammates named Bob Miller. They were both pitchers and roommates!

pop the question. Hudler followed the advice, and it worked.
Jennifer and Rex were married the following year.

Eight years after coaching Hudler in courtship, Ripken
gave his old friends something else to remember him by. The
Angels were the Orioles' opponents as Ripken broke Lou Gehrig's
consecutive-game record, playing game number 2,131. Hudler
was in the lineup at second base for the Angels that night and
watched his friend enjoy his finest moment. When Ripken's former infield mate returned to
the clubhouse after the game
that night, a baseball bat was
awaiting him in his locker.
Ripken had been waiting for
the opportunity to razz
Hudler about how their
careers had played out, and
in the spirit of their friendship, he took this moment to
do just that. On the bat,
Ripken wrote this message:

*"Rex, you know it's
been a long time since we
broke in, your going ahead
of me in the draft, until this
date. Right now I'm feeling like
you when you strike out with
the bases loaded:* VISIBLY
SHAKEN – Cal Ripken Jr.,
9/6/95"

DID YOU KNOW?

*Hall of Fame pitcher Hoyt
Wilhelm fought in the Battle
of the Bulge in WWII,
suffering wounds that led
to a permanently crooked neck.*

KNUCKLING UNDER

F ew things in baseball are more humbling to a Major League batter than being retired by a pitcher who throws 50 mph. But occasionally, when they are faced with the prospect of hitting a knuckleball, it can be a common occurrence.

Steve Sparks is a pitcher who has made a living with the Milwaukee Brewers, Anaheim Angels, Detroit Tigers, and Oakland A's by throwing the knuckleball, making him quite unusual among his peers. During the mid-1900s, knuckleball pitchers were common on Major League rosters, but in the new millennium, Sparks is the only true knuckleball specialist who pitches regularly on a big-league team.

"The biggest thing about a knuckleball is it's hard to throw for strikes," says Sparks. "The one thing I've learned is that I have to stay real patient with it and just realize that I am maybe just one pitch—one good knuckleball—away from a double play. I have to stick with it."

Such an approach was key for Sparks as he progressed beyond the scouts and baseball-management personnel who doubted a pure knuckleball pitcher could succeed in modern-day baseball. But nothing could have prepared Sparks for what he would encounter in spring training of 1994.

Sparks was close to earning a big-league roster spot with Milwaukee, after having a solid spring training. A few weeks before camp broke for the start of the regular season, the

Brewers team was visited by a group
of motivational speakers called
Radical Reality. Members of the
group exhibited impressive feats of
strength—bending iron bars with
their hands, ripping telephone
books in half, and inflating hot-water bottles like balloons,
until they burst, before presenting inspirational messages to the
Brewers team members.

The day after Radical Reality's presentation, Sparks and
a few teammates tried the phone-book feat with the Phoenix
Yellow Pages. Sparks had the massive book almost torn in half
when he dislocated his left shoulder in the effort. The injury put
him out for several weeks and became a source of mockery from
the media. Sparks' story was written up in *Sports Illustrated* and
carried by countless newspapers across the country. Even today,
he is constantly reminded that it's a story that still has life.

"To this day, going into Boston and New York, they [the
media] get such a kick out of the story that I am constantly
asked to sign telephone books there," Sparks says.

DID YOU KNOW?

Four baseball Hall of Famers
once played basketball for the
Harlem Globetrotters: Bob
Gibson, Ferguson Jenkins,
Lou Brock, and Satchel Paige.

BASEBALL'S ALL-LAW & ORDER TEAM

WALT BOND

WILLIE MIRANDA

DAVE JUSTICE

CRAIG COUNSELL

TOM LAWLESS

VANCE LAW

JOE JUDGE

DH - **LEE BALES**

P - **VERN LAW**
GEORGE CASE

JOHNNY BENCH

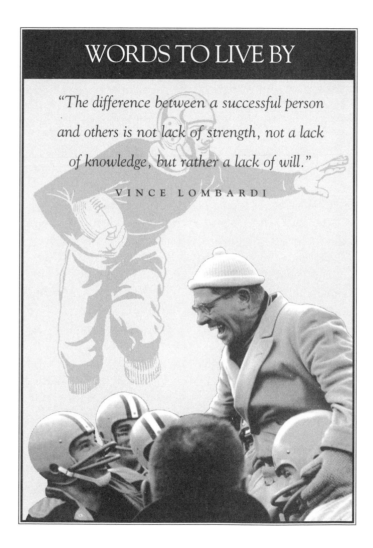

WORDS TO LIVE BY

"The difference between a successful person and others is not lack of strength, not a lack of knowledge, but rather a lack of will."

VINCE LOMBARDI

TOUCHING ALL THE BASES: FRED #1

H all of Fame manager John McGraw led the New York Giants to ten National League championships during the early 1900s. But until his death, McGraw bemoaned the "one that got away." He told reporters, "I won eleven pennants. Ten are in the book, but the eleventh was stolen from me in a National League meeting room."

McGraw was referring to a series of events in 1908, when the Giants entered the home stretch of the season in a tense three-way race with the Pittsburgh Pirates and Chicago Cubs. The Giants led the Cubs by only six percentage points when the two played at the Polo Grounds on September 23. Twenty thousand fans packed the stadium in hopes of watching their beloved Giants move one step closer to the pennant. They certainly did not expect to see New York's rookie infielder Fred Merkle be the deciding factor.

Merkle hadn't played in a game all season and was inserted into the lineup only because starting first baseman Fred Tenney was ill, forcing him to miss his only game of the season.

The game was tied 1-1 in the bottom of the ninth, when Merkle got a base hit to put runners at first and third with two outs. Giants star Moose McCormick was at third base, just 90 feet away from scoring the winning run. Merkle was at first base, with hopes of being part of a heroic ending. What happened next has never really been settled, but accounts of the game let us know it was a wild finish.

The Giants' Al Bridwell was the next batter. He hit a line drive to center field, and McCormick trotted home with the apparent winning run. The crowd went wild, streaming onto the field and creating a scene of mayhem.

But Cubs Hall of Fame second baseman Johnny Evers knew that the game was not necessarily over. Amid the chaos around him, Evers frantically called for Cubs center fielder Art Hoffman to throw him the ball. At the same time, Evers was shouting to the umpire that Merkle had never touched second base. Evidently, in his haste to get off the field and avoid being mobbed by fans, Merkle, upon seeing the ball drop into center field, headed straight for the dugout rather than head to second base. This was common in a game-winning situation such as this one, but according to baseball rules, Merkle could be

DID YOU KNOW?

- 1/8 was the uniform number worn by 3'7", 65-pound Eddie Gaedel during a pinch-hit appearance for St. Louis Browns in 1951.

- 00 was the uniform number worn by pitcher Omar Oliveras to reflect his initials.

forced out at second base if any fielder tagged the base prior to Merkle's touching the base. Such a force-out would nullify the run.

Hoffman threw the ball toward second base, where a mob of fans had encircled Evers and other players still on the field. No one is sure who caught Hoffman's throw, but players reported afterward that Giants pitcher Joe McGinnity wrestled the ball away from whomever had it, and promptly threw it into the stands.

Merkle, now aware of his error, was now frantically attempting to get back to touch second base, while Chicago fans were draped all over him, trying to prevent him from getting to the bag. By this time, someone had evidently tossed a new ball to second base. When Merkle finally made it to second, Evers was standing on the bag, holding the new ball. Umpire Bob Emslie had already retreated to the dressing room, so the remaining umpire, Hank O'Day, was left to make the call, surrounded by frenzied players and fans demanding a decision. O'Day called Merkle out and declared the game a tie.

In the aftermath, both teams protested the ruling to the National League president, Harry Pulliam, who called a special league meeting. It was determined that the ruling on the field would stand, and that, if necessary, a playoff would be held after the season.

The playoff was necessary because the Giants and the Cubs finished the season in a dead heat, tied for first place. On October 8, 35,000 fans—the largest in baseball history at the time—filled the stands at the Polo Grounds to watch the Giants and Cubs play one game for the pennant. To Fred Merkle's lifelong regret, the Giants lost 4-2 and with it, lost the pennant. Fred Merkle's place in baseball history was assured.

DID YOU KNOW?

The game was called "Base Ball" until the 1930s

BASEBALL'S ALL-FORECAST TEAM

CURT FLOOD

JOHN HALE

JAKE FREEZE

ALVIN DARK

TIM RAINES

NIPPY JONES

KEN CLOUDE
MARK CLEAR
JAMIE EASTERLY
DAVE FROST
ERNIE GUST
DAVE WEATHERS
RICH GALE
STORM DAVIS

J.T. SNOW

DH - GEORGE WINTER

HARRY BRIGHT

ESCAPING BLAME: FRED #2

Four years after Fred Merkle took the blame for costing the Giants the pennant, another Fred was blamed for costing the Giants the 1912 World Series.

Fred Snodgrass' mistake was dubbed the "$100,000 muff," referring to the money the Giants lost in World Series bonus money. The team actually lost $39,000—still a considerable sum at the time.

Snodgrass' error came in the final game of the series, which pitted the Giants against the Boston Red Sox. With the series tied at three games apiece, New York led Boston 2-1 in the top of the tenth inning of the decisive game 7. Boston pinch-hitter Clyde Engle hit a fly ball to center field. Snodgrass went for the ball, but became distracted when a fan threw a bottle at him. Snodgrass missed the ball, and Engle was safe at first base. After Harry Hooper flied out, Steve Yerkes walked, putting runners at first and second. Tris Speaker then singled to right, allowing Engle to cross the plate and tie the score at 2-2. Next, Duffy Lewis walked, and Larry Gardner followed with a

sacrifice fly to bring in Yerkes with the winning run. The Giants didn't score in their half of the tenth, and the Red Sox won the World Series.

Snodgrass was blamed for the Giants woes, even though he rejected taking responsibility for his team's fate. "I certainly dropped that ball," he would say 40 years later. "But it happened on the first man up in the tenth. I did not let in the run that gave the championship to Boston."

Some Giants fans were willing to let Snodgrass off the hook. They felt it was not his error, but rather

William "Dummy" Hoy, was a baseball star in the early 1900s. He was deaf. Because of Hoy's inability to hear the umpire's pitch call while he was batting, umpires around the league instituted the use of hand signals to signify balls and strikes. The practice has been a central part of baseball ever since.

another muff that took place in the same inning that truly cost the Giants the series. Prior to Speaker's belting his game-tying single, he hit a short foul pop that should have been caught. Instead, it fell harmlessly between two Giants fielders. Those two Giants who missed the ball were catcher Chief Meyers, and, you may have guessed it, first baseman Fred Merkle. Amazingly, Merkle escaped the majority of the blame for this one.

BASEBALL'S ALL-INTERNATIONAL TEAM

Lineup Card

Team __ALL INTERNATIONAL__

Pos.	Player
C	JIM FRENCH
1B	JOE HAGUE
2B	JEFF KENT
SS	MIGUEL CAIRO
3B	KELLY PARIS
OF	CLYDE MILAN
OF	STEVE GIBRALTER
OF	TRENIDAD HUBBARD
OF	BILL ROMAN
DH	TIM IRELAND
P	JIM BRITTON
P	PAUL MOSKAU
P	ISRAEL SANCHEZ
P	MARK PORTUGAL
P	ANDREW LORRAINE
P	ALEX MADRID

WRONG-WAY ROY

The Rose Bowl is known as the "Granddaddy" of all bowl games. It has been the scene of some of college football's greatest individual performances, most amazing plays, and historic finishes.

But in the lore of college football, one play stands above the rest. It occurred at the 1929 Rose Bowl game, between the University of California at Berkley and Georgia Tech, and it was one of the most spectacular—and most bizarre—runs in football history.

In the late 1920s, the Rose Bowl was the only postseason college football game. Millions of fans around the country listened to the game on the radio. Every major city's newspaper covered the action, and in the aftermath, football fans across the country would talk about the game for days, if not weeks. Thus, the events of Jan. 1, 1929, made California's Roy Riegels the most talked-about athlete in America. But it was not exactly the kind of recognition the young man wanted.

Early in the second quarter, with the score 0-0, Tech had the ball on its own 20. Tech halfback Stumpy Thomason took the snap and swung wide to his left, behind good blocking. Near the 30-yard line, he was hit by two California tacklers. The football squirted out of his hands and bounced along the grass.

California junior Roy Riegels, who was playing roving center on defense, was in position to make the play. "As the ball fell away from Thomason, I picked it up and ran," Riegels later remembered. "The defense could do that in those days. I started in the right direction but made a complete horseshoe turn after going four or five yards—when I saw two players coming at me from the right. In pivoting to get away, I completely lost my bearings. I wasn't out of my head at all. I hadn't been hurt. I just headed the wrong way."

As Riegels galloped downfield, unknowingly headed toward scoring a touchdown for the opponent, alert teammate Benny Lom, a halfback for the Golden Bears, reacted quickly, and began chasing Riegels. As Lom gained on Riegels, he shouted frantically, "Stop! Stop! You're going the wrong way!"

Riegels, however, thought his teammate wanted the ball so he could score the touchdown.

"As I neared the goal line, I could hear Benny yelling for me to throw him the ball. Shucks, I wasn't going to throw it to him after that run," Riegels would explain. "There was nothing going through my mind except that I wanted to make a touchdown. I can't even think of a decent alibi. I just bounced out with the ball, saw a pair of goalposts, and headed for them."

Lom finally caught up to Riegels, grabbed his hand, and spun him around. But by this time, the two men were standing on the one-yard line. As they looked back toward the distant

Tech goal line, Riegels realized something was terribly wrong. But before he could make the slightest move, Tech end Frank Waddey plowed into him. Then a wave of Tech players rolled over him, driving him into the end zone as Lom stepped aside.

Referee Herb Dana ruled the ball dead on the one-yard line.

Teammates tried to console Riegels, who sat on the ground for some time, holding his head in his hands. Even some Georgia Tech players patted him on the shoulders. California coach Nibs Price had compassion on his player and left Riegels in the game.

On the ensuing play, which Cal launched from its own one, Riegels centered the ball accurately to punter Lom. But Tech tackle Vance Maree leaped to block the kick. In the ensuing scramble, Cal halfback Stan Barr was the last to touch the ball before it bounced out of the end zone. Tech was awarded a safety—and a 2-0 lead. Those points proved decisive in the game.

Tech added a touchdown in the third quarter but missed the extra point. California scored in the final two minutes but would score no more. When the game ended 8-7, Riegels was marked for life. He came to be forever known as "Wrong Way Riegels."

Even though Riegels was elected team captain the following season—and earned All-America honors, the moniker stuck. Sponsorship offers came in for upside-down cakes, backward walkathons, ties with stripes going the wrong way, and a number of similar products.

Under the weight of humiliation that could have crushed him, Riegels turned his place in history into a position of responsibility. The man called "the smartest boy on the squad" by his coach was able to laugh at himself throughout his life; he learned to enjoy his infamy.

"Sometimes," he once quipped, "even my ten-year-old son calls me Wrong Way Riegels."

DID YOU KNOW?

Helmets were not mandatory in pro football until 1944.

In 1980, NBC experimented by televising the New York Jets-Miami Dolphins game without any announcers. The broadcast used only sounds from the field and from the stadium's public address system.

Pete Gogolak became the NFL's first soccer-style place kicker in 1964.

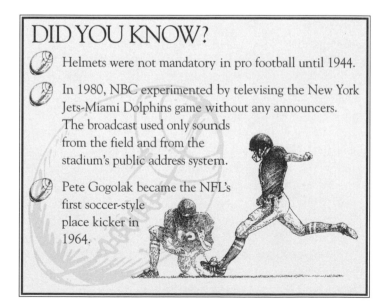

THE TWELFTH MAN

Sometimes a college athlete's excitement and intensity get the best of him. When it happens on a national stage, he might have to live with the results for a long time. Such is the case with Alabama football player Tommy Lewis.

In the 1954 Cotton Bowl, the Crimson Tide of Alabama faced the mighty Rice Owls in a game that would be remembered more for one play than the final score.

During the first quarter, Rice halfback Dicky Maegle took a handoff and sprinted down the right sideline, in front of the Alabama bench, on his way to an apparent 95-yard touchdown run. That's when Lewis, an Alabama fullback made his infamous play.

Standing on the sideline, Lewis watched as Maegle avoided one 'Bama tackler after another, then broke into the clear. As adrenaline surged through him, Lewis reacted. With Maegle 57 yards into his run, Lewis charged from the sideline and tackled him. Maegle, not expecting the hit, went down in a heap. Lewis, himself so stunned at what he had done, scrambled quickly back to the Alabama bench and tried to act as if nothing had happened.

"I kept telling myself, 'I didn't do it. I didn't do it.'" he said later. "But I knew I did."

It was a play the 75,000 spectators and live national television audience had never seen before. Nor had the officials, who awarded an automatic touchdown to Maegle.

Lewis told reporters afterward that his reaction came about because he was "too full of Alabama." While no one ever blamed Lewis for Alabama's 28-6 loss, his feelings of guilt were so deep, that he apologized to Maegle after the game and cried openly in the locker room, saying, "I don't think I'll ever get over it. I know I'm going to hear about this for the rest of my life."

Lewis was right. Maegle turned in the greatest single performance in the history of the Cotton Bowl, gaining 261 yards rushing on only 11 carries and three touchdowns—yet the focus of the game from coast to coast was Lewis' tackle.

Following the game, Ed Sullivan invited Lewis and Maegle to appear live on *The Ed Sullivan Show*. But when he ran short on time, Sullivan wound up interviewing only Lewis and never said a word to Maegle. It seemed that Lewis had become a sort of hero for being so inspired by the team spirit that led to his memorable tackle.

Sullivan apologized to Maegle and invited him back to the show to appear by himself. But the slighted halfback declined, saying he was too busy studying for exams.

In spite of Lewis' fame, he always felt haunted by the incident. Many years after the game, he wrote to Maegle to ask for advice on how to live with his infamy. Maegle wrote back, advising Lewis to try to see the humor in the situation. But Lewis found it difficult to do so. He would never again watch a Cotton Bowl when Alabama played, for fear of seeing his personal nightmare replayed.

DID YOU KNOW?

The first Super Bowl, in 1967, was called the "AFL-NFL World Championship Game." It was held at the L.A. Coliseum, was not sold-out, and was broadcast by both CBS and NBC. Ticket prices for the game ranged from $6-12, and a total of 338 media credentials were issued to the game. The price of a 30-second television commercial was $42,000. By contrast, tickets to the 1999 Super Bowl were priced at $325; 30-second commercials went for $1.6 million. The game was covered by 2,300 media members, broadcast to 800 million people worldwide, covering 180 countries and 24 languages.

WORDS TO LIVE BY

"The answers to these questions will determine your success or failure. 1) Can people trust me to do what's right? 2) Am I committed to doing my best? 3) Do I care about other people and show it? If the answers to these questions are yes, there is no way you can fail."

LOU HOLTZ
head football coach, University of South Carolina

"It is your response to winning and losing that makes you a winner or a loser."

HARRY SHEEHY
athletic director, Williams College

A WELL-HEELED GOLFER

C anadian-born Moe Norman won seven consecutive Canadian PGA championships from 1979 to 1985. He was notable for his accomplishments—and his unconventional swing, which included an abbreviated backswing.

Norman was also a top golf consultant. A month's worth of personalized instruction with him cost as much as $100,000. But many golfers have said the price was well worth it, because of his unusual prowess off the tee. In fact, in an interview in 1996, Norman claimed to have played every hole since 1989 using the same tee. He added that he hadn't hit a ball out of bounds in 11 years.

True or not, such stories were a part of what made Norman's persona so engaging. He was thought of as a bit of a free spirit, and was as much an entertainer as a golfer. He often clowned with the galleries and played up to them.

He was known to tee balls atop such unusual items as Coke bottles, then hit picture-perfect drives down the fairway. Other golfers, such as long-time PGA and Senior Tour favorite Juan "Chi Chi" Rodriguez have also wowed crowds with similar stunts in exhibitions. But no other pro is on record for having teed off the way Norman did on one memorable occasion, when he used a woman's high-heeled shoe!

DIZZY TIZZY

Dizzy Dean was one of the great characters in baseball. His country humor and innocence endeared him to the press and fans alike. Dean was a star pitcher for the St. Louis Cardinals in the 1930s and '40s, before heading to the broadcast booth.

Dean was a 30-game winner for the Cards, but is best known for a slew of memorable one-liners.

Once, speaking about the Negro League pitching great Satchel Paige, Dean said, "If Satch and I were pitching on the same team, we'd cinch the pennant by July 4 and go fishing until World Series time."

Dizzy didn't pitch with Paige, but for a time, he did team up with his brother Paul Dean on the St. Louis Cardinals staff. Once, after Dizzy had pitched a one-hitter in the first game of a doubleheader, Paul went one better by tossing a no-hitter in the nightcap. Following the game, Dizzy told the press, "Shucks, if I'd known Paul was gonna pitch a no-hitter, I'da pitched one too."

Often, Dean's words rung true. Once, during the close of the 1934 season, Dean had grown leery of the quality of the Cardinals pitching staff – excluding himself and Paul. With the World Series looming, Dean was asked how the Cardinals would fare against the

Did you know... that former outfielder Carlos May is the only athlete ever to wear his birthday on his uniform? May, who was born on May 17, wore number 17 during his 10 years with the White Sox, New York Yankees and California Angels from 1968-1977. With his number situated in the center on the back of his jersey, just under his last name running across the back of his shoulders, his jersey read "May 17".

Detroit Tigers. "Me and Paul," Dean replied, "will win two games apiece."

While the words may not have seemed like a confidence-booster for his teammates, they did prove to be prophetic. The Cards won games 1, 2, 6, and 7—all games pitched by the Dean brothers, to take the Series 4 games to 3.

Dean also became known for his verbal bloopers. During one game in the 1934 World Series he was hit on the head by a fly ball. Some time later, he was asked how he felt. He told the press he was fine, explaining, "The doctors X-rayed my head, and found nothing."

As a broadcaster, Dean wrapped up his commentary of a 1-0 game he had called by telling his audience, "The game was closer than the score indicated."

Dean was also accused of serving as a poor role model for students of the English language because of his poor use of grammar and diction. Retorted Dean, "A lot of people who don't say ain't, ain't eatin!"

Later, during an interview with a British reporter, Dean was asked, "Mr. Dean, don't you know the king's English?"

"Sure I do," Dizzy replied after a moment's reflection, "and so is the queen."

RACING ON FUMES

Wilbur Shaw was one of the early superstars of auto racing. In the 1930s and '40s, he was the big name in Indy-style racing circles. He became known not only for his driving ability, but also his penchant for taking risks—risks that usually paid off. He seemed to have a knack for knowing just what he had to do to win. The 1937 Indianapolis 500 is one example.

At Indy that year, Shaw had a three-mile lead on second-place driver Ralph Hepburn, with 35 laps to go. The lead amounted to more than one lap on the 2.5-mile oval. Shaw seemed to be coasting to another victory at the famed Brickyard.

Then the unthinkable happened: Shaw sprung a leak. His Maserati 8CTF began leaking oil at a rate that threatened to take him out of the race. Told by his pit crew that he was one minute and fourteen seconds ahead of Hepburn, Shaw immediately calculated in his head how much he could afford to slow down to conserve oil and still win.

Shaw cut his speed. Hepburn quickly began to catch up. Soon, he had regained one lap's worth of the distance he had fallen behind. It was now a tight race.

Shaw began to rethink his math, wondering if he had calculated correctly. With every second, Hepburn made up more ground. On the last turn of the final lap, Hepburn came even with Shaw and began nosing ahead. It looked like Shaw would lose the race.

But just as Hepburn came alongside of him, Shaw accelerated, hoping there was enough oil for one last push. His Maserati gave one last chug. Then the engine gasped and quit—just as the car crossed the finish line. Amazingly, with hardly more than a drop of oil left in his engine, Shaw edged Hepburn in what was the closest race in Indianapolis 500 history—a 2.16-second margin of victory.

THE TWO-TIMER

Dale Holman was a top minor-league player for a handful of teams. The outfielder was the seemingly eternal prospect, the guy who always hit well at every level of the minors but was never in the right place to get a shot at the big leagues. He is also the central figure of one baseball's strangest stories.

On June 30, 1986, Holman was playing for the Syracuse Chiefs, then the AAA affiliate of the Toronto Blue Jays. The Chiefs were taking on the Richmond Braves, the AAA affiliate of the Atlanta Braves, in an International League game.

Early in the contest, Holman came to bat with two men on base—and promptly laced a double, scoring both runners and giving Syracuse the lead. A short time later, the game was suspended and scheduled to be completed at a later date. Following the game, Holman was released by the Chiefs, then signed by Richmond.

Several days later, when the suspended game was scheduled to be completed, Holman was chosen to play outfield for the Braves.

Holman singled and doubled in his two trips to the plate for the Braves that night, as the suspended game was completed. When the final box score was compiled, it showed a very rare statistical oddity: Dale Holman had collected a hit for two opposing teams in the same game!

HELLO AGAIN

As the 1987 Major League Baseball season drew to a close, several teams in the pennant chase jockeyed to make key trades that could help them overcome their competition. A key pinch hitter, another strong arm in the bullpen, or a late-inning defensive replacement could help a team get to the top.

Right-handed relief pitcher Dickie Noles was one player many teams attempted to pry away from the Chicago Cubs. Late in the season, the Detroit Tigers swung a deal to bring Noles to the Motor City. In return, the Cubs would receive a player to be named later from the Tigers. Ultimately, Noles pitched in just four games for the Tigers, who didn't make it to the postseason.

When the season was over, management for the Tigers and Cubs got together to discuss completing the trade and determining "the player to be named later." At the end of the negotiations, they decided that Noles would be that player. So, Noles eventually left Detroit and reported back to the Cubs.

What it all meant was that in the course of a just few weeks, Dickie Noles became the first player in history to be traded for himself!

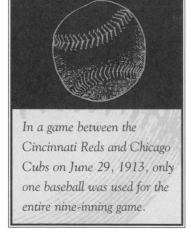

In a game between the Cincinnati Reds and Chicago Cubs on June 29, 1913, only one baseball was used for the entire nine-inning game.

SAY WHAT?

"When I got traded here it turned my career around 360 degrees."

ED JOVANOVSKI

NHL all-star defenseman, on his improvement
since being traded to Vancouver in 1999.

DID YOU KNOW?

Current NASCAR driver Dave Marcis has been known to drive while wearing wingtip shoes.

THAT'S WHY THEY CALL IT "THE SHOW"

I n 1913, during a late-spring baseball game, the New York Giants and the Philadelphia Phillies were locked in a defensive battle. Well into the 10th inning, neither team had been able to score. And that's when an umpire took center stage.

The Giants had runners on base as Frank McCormick came up to pinch-hit, with a chance to win the game. As McCormick stepped into the batter's box, home-plate umpire Bill Klem turned his back to the plate and faced the stands to announce the change in batters to the crowd. While his back was turned, Klem didn't see Phillies star pitcher Grover Cleveland Alexander throw a fastball that McCormick promptly hit into left field to drive in the apparent game-winning run.

As Giants base-runner Fred Merkle trotted home from third base, Klem was still in the midst of the batter introduction. When Merkle touched the plate, both teams jogged toward the locker rooms. McCormick was basking in his game-winning heroics as he made his way past the press toward his locker—when Klem apprehended him.

The umpire brought McCormick to the batter's box, and then ordered both teams back onto the field. He explained that the ball had not yet been put back into play during McCormick's introduction, which, he added, was still not complete. Therefore, neither the hit nor the run counted, so the game wasn't over.

Thus, both teams took their respective positions and waited for Klem to clear his throat and complete the longest introduction of a pinch-hitter in baseball history. When he was finished, play finally resumed.

This time, Alexander induced McCormick into a ground-out, and the score remained tied at 0-0. The two teams played another inning without scoring, then the game was officially called on account of darkness after eleven innings, going into the record books as a 0-0 tie.

CATCH ME IF YOU CAN

Throughout the years, many crafty baseball pitchers have discovered ways to doctor the baseball to make it move unusually when they throw a pitch. Some have been caught with such illegal substances and items as petroleum jelly, thumbtacks, sandpaper, and various other odds and ends.

One pitcher who umpires were certain was doctoring the ball was Don Sutton. Sutton, who played for the Dodgers, Brewers, and Angels, compiled 323 victories over his career. Yet many felt much of his success resulted from what he did to the ball before he threw it.

One night in 1978, with Sutton on the mound for the Dodgers, umpire Doug Harvey found a foreign substance on the ball during an opponent's at bat. Harvey promptly tossed Sutton from the game. Sutton was livid. He refuted Harvey's claim—and threatened to sue Harvey and the other umpires if they ejected him from the game. To placate matters, Harvey informed Sutton that he was being removed from the game because he had thrown a doctored ball. They could not definitively say that Sutton himself had doctored the ball.

Because umpires had never yet been successful in catching Sutton in the act, they were hesitant to waste time looking for something illegal. On this occasion, Sutton took everything in stride. When one of the umpiring crew went to the mound to search Sutton's glove for a foreign substance, he instead found a note from the pitcher. It read: "You're getting warm, but it is not here."

BASEBALL'S ALL-FOOD TEAM

Y ou've probably heard about various sports experts' "All-Time, All-Star teams." It's a tough task to pick the nine best baseball stars who've ever played the game. Pundits and fans alike could argue for days on whether Sandy Koufax or Cy Young is the greatest pitcher ever. But there isn't as much argument about Major League Baseball's "All-Food Team." Check out the roster and see what you think . . .

Mgr - HERMAN FRANKS & MAYO SMITH

ZACH WHEAT
BILLY BEAN

JIM RICE   DARRYL
GINGER BEAUMONT   STRAWBERRY

BOBBY   GENE
WINE   LEEK

BOB VEALE
CHET   DAVID CONE   JOHNNY
LEMON   PETE HAMM   ROMANO
              MARK LEMONGELLO
              TERRY CORNUTT
              STEVE CURRY
              STEVE GERKIN
              BOB LEMON
              JOSE LIMA

DH - DUKE CARMEL

JOHNNY OATES

THE IMPOSTER

Rosie Ruiz was not the first person caught cheating in a marathon, but as far as anyone knows, she was the first to be caught cheating in two marathons.

Ruiz was a complete unknown when she crossed the finish line at the 1980 Boston Marathon—as the third-fastest woman marathon runner (2:31:56)—in history. But race officials of the Boston Athletic Association immediately knew something was not right with Ruiz's finish. First, none of the checkpoint officials had seen her running on the course. Second, none of the other top-finishing women had seen her pass them. Third, two Harvard students who were spectators in the crowd that day told officials they had seen Ruiz enter the race from the crowd about a half mile from the finish line.

When she met the frantic press corps after her remarkable "finish," Ruiz only hurt her attempt at getting away with her scheme. When asked about her split times, she told the media she could not recall any of them. Further, it was clear from her answers that she was not sure what split times were.

With the BAA officials huddled together, trying to decide about whether or not to award Ruiz the champion's laurel wreath, skeptical media members did some figuring of their own. Several writers began checking background information on Ruiz. They learned that she had cheated in the New York Marathon the previous year, in the race that had supposedly qualified her for Boston. A photographer told the press that she had spotted Ruiz taking a short cut by subway during the New York race, and that Ruiz never crossed the finish line. Still, Ruiz had been credited with running a Boston-qualifying time of 2:56:29. Embarrassed New York race officials checked videotapes of the finish and could not find Ruiz ever crossing the finish line. So they eventually voided her time.

In the aftermath of the Boston race, while officials fussed over what to do, Ruiz hit the television talk show circuit. For an entire week, America was learning of this "novice" runner who won the grandest marathon in the world. In interviews, Ruiz told of how her resting heart rate was 76 beats per minute —more than 20 beats per minute more than that of world-class runners. She said she had been training for only about a year and a half, that she did not know what interval training was, and that she could not recall what Massachusetts towns she had run through. But Ruiz was resolute. Even in the moment of her disqualification, she maintained she had completed the entire 26.2-mile race. Boston officials had no way of proving she had not, but decided that her story didn't match up and that the evidence pointed to the fact that Ruiz could not have run or won the race. So, they took her crown away and presented the first prize to Canadian Jacqueline Gareau.

When all the commotion was settled, Ruiz had enjoyed her "15 minutes of fame," and her theatrics were commemorated with a T-shirt that became a popular prop for running clubs around the U.S. Emblazoned on the shirt were the words ROSIE RUIZ TRACK CLUB; the logo was a New York City subway token.

GETTING THE SIGNALS CROSSED

Former Cleveland Browns coach and owner Paul Brown was one of the most respected men in all of pro football. He was known as an innovator who left an indelible mark on the game. One of Brown's innovations was the use of electronics to send in plays from the coach on the sideline to the quarterback in the huddle. In 1956, Brown had a radio receiver installed in the helmet of his quarterback, Otto Graham. Brown was so excited about the advanced technology that he told the media about using the receiver.

In October of the 1956 season, the New York Giants hosted the Browns at Yankee Stadium. The Giants had learned of Brown's use of the radio receiver—and found a way to tune into the frequency Cleveland was using. They were able to hear Brown's transmission to his quarterback, and they intercepted the plays he called for his offense. The plays were then relayed to the Giants defense, which completely shut down the Browns offense.

Late in the game, Brown realized what was happening, so he ditched the transmission idea. He went back to the old way of sending in plays, by a messenger player. It proved too late, however, as the Giants beat the favored Browns by the score of 21-9.

GETTING CROSS ABOUT SIGNALS

Oakland Raiders owner Al Davis has a long-standing reputation for doing just about anything to give his team an edge. At times the edge came on the field; at other times the edge was psychological.

For example, during the early days of the American Football League, the rumor spread that Davis had hidden microphones in the visiting team's locker room at the Oakland Coliseum. At halftime of a game between Oakland and San Diego (with the Chargers losing), San Diego coach Harland Svare—aware of the rumor—looked up at a light fixture in the middle of the locker room, shook his fist, and said, "Darn you, Al Davis, Darn you! I know you're up there!"

THE LONG AND SHORT OF IT

Point guard Avery Johnson is one of the true success stories in the NBA. After being cut by numerous teams, and being told he was too small to make it in the league, Johnson survived and led the San Antonio Spurs to the NBA title in 1999. But Johnson has had his share of moments he would rather forget along the way. Including one when he was a rookie with the Seattle SuperSonics.

Johnson was a backup, whose role was to come off the bench to give the Sonics a few minutes of up-tempo energy on the court. He also provided the team with some comic relief. But no moment was funnier to his teammates than this one.

Johnson had planned on bringing some levity to the team one night before a game. So he came out of the team's locker room for warm-ups with his uniform shorts on backward. "I put my pants on backwards," Johnson recalls, "and I was joking. I said to my teammates, 'You guys think I'm going to go out there on the court [for the game] with my pants on backwards, don't you?' Then I went to get taped, and I forgot to turn my pants around."

By game time, Johnson's mind was focused on what was taking place on the court. His shorts were "out of sight, out of mind." Things stayed that way until Sonics coach Bernie Bickerstaff called for Johnson to go into the game.

"When Bernie put me in the game, I had my pants on backwards," says Johnson. "And I was wondering why everybody was laughing."

Not only did Johnson's teammates recognize his fashion statement, but so did most of the crowd. Johnson still didn't know that he was the butt of the joke until his coach called time-out to rescue his point guard from further embarrassment.

"Bernie called a twenty-second time-out, kind walked over [to me], and I didn't understand what was wrong," Johnson says. "Everybody was crying-laughing. They had tears in their eyes. Our trainer, Frank Fratato, was coming over with three

towels and they put them all around my body. Everybody said, 'Put your pants on the right way.' So I had to do it right then at half-court of the Summit Arena in Houston."

Says Johnson of the moment that made the NBA blooper reels: "It was just embarrassing. But it was funny, and things like that happen in the NBA. That's the most embarrassing thing that's happened to me."

THIS SPUD'S FOR YOU

E ven the minor leagues have their share
of amazing stories. Perhaps the most
infamous occurred in 1987 and involved a
25-year-old second-string catcher named
Dave Bresnahan. Bresnahan played for the
Williamsport (Pennsylvania) Bills of the Class
AA Eastern League. The Bills were playing in
a meaningless late-season home game at the
end of August when Bresnahan decided to liven things up.

Before the game, Bresnahan had holed up in his locker
and spent several minutes peeling and sculpting a potato into
the shape of a baseball. Bresnahan knew he would be behind
the plate during that day's game, and he waited for the oppor-
tune time to put his plan into action. In the fifth inning, he
found his opportunity.

With a runner on third base, Bresnahan pulled the potato
from his back pocket and concealed it in his mitt. When the
pitcher threw to the
plate, Bresnahan
grabbed the potato
with his bare hand,
caught the pitch, then
threw the potato wildly
past his third baseman.
Bresnahan was hop-
ing the base runner
would think he

made an errant pick-off throw, and would head for home. The play worked just as the catcher had planned. The runner at third scampered home, where Bresnahan was waiting with the baseball and tagged him out.

Ample confusion followed the play. While both teams tried to sort out the confusion, an umpire retrieved the potato from the third-base line, and recognizing what had happened, awarded the runner home, due to Bresnahan's deception.

The following day, Bresnahan was fined by his manager, then released by the Bills' parent club, the Cleveland Indians, for actions they considered to be an affront to the game's integrity.

Although his four-year professional baseball career was over, Bresnahan became an instant celebrity. He fielded interview requests from around the world and was named the 1987 Sports Person of the Year by Chicago Tribune columnist Bob Verdi.

In 1988, the Williamsport Bills held a Dave Bresnahan Day, bringing the catcher back and retiring his uniform number, 59. In addressing the more than 4,000 fans attending, Bresnahan said, "Lou Gehrig had to play in 2,130 consecutive games and hit .340 for his number to be retired, and all I had to do was bat .140 and throw a potato."

The potato, incidentally, was salvaged from a trash can after the game by a teen boy and offered to the National Baseball Hall of Fame and Museum in Cooperstown, New York. Officials reportedly showed little interest in acquiring it. So baseball's most famous spud now resides in a specimen jar at the Baseball Reliquary.

As for Bresnahan, he is now a stockbroker.

STAND BY YOUR MAN

Paul "Bear" Bryant was the winningest coach of his era, totaling more than 300 victories and establishing a legacy at the University of Alabama. One day after practice in the mid-1960s, Bryant called a team meeting. He felt it was time to lay down more-stringent discipline guidelines for his team. He gathered his players around and told them, "This is a class operation. I want your shoes to be shined. I want you to have a tie on, get your hair cut, and keep a crease in your pants. I also want you to go to class. I don't want no dumbbells on this team. If there is a dumbbell in the room, I wish he would stand up."

Suddenly, star quarterback Joe Namath rose to his feet. Startled, the Bear looked at his leader and said, "Joe, how come you're standing up? You ain't dumb."

Namath responded, "Coach, I just hate like the devil for you to be standing up there all by yourself!"

The Baltimore Colts found future Hall of Fame quarterback, Johnny Unitas, playing semipro football for the Bluefield Rams in 1955, after he had been cut by the Pittsburgh Steelers. Once unwanted, he is now regarded as the best quarterback in football history.

PERISTROIKA?

In 1972, the Canadians and the Russians faced off in a historic hockey series called the Summit Series. It was a match-up between Canada's finest NHL stars, and the best of the Soviet Red Army team— their Olympians. The series will long be remembered in Canada for Paul Henderson's series-winning goal, which made him a national hero and household name throughout Canada.

However, few are familiar with some of the diplomatic challenges that came with the series, at a time in which Soviet political relations with the West were a bit icy. The tension carried onto the rinks—and the events that surrounded the series.

While visiting Moscow to play the Russians in the midst of the series, the Canadian hockey team was assigned a hotel room that they suspected had been bugged.

Recalls Canadian superstar goal-scorer, Phil Esposito, then of the NHL's Boston Bruins, "We searched the room for microphones. In the center of the room, we found a funny-looking, round piece of metal embedded in the floor, under the rug. We figured we had found the bug. We dug it out of the floor and heard a crash beneath us. We had released the anchor to the chandelier in the ceiling below."

WELCOME TO THE CIRCUS

B ill Veeck was one of the most imaginative promoters in baseball. Some called him a genius. Others called him eccentric. Either way, he certainly left his mark on the game.

Perhaps the one day that best demonstrated Veeck's Barnumesque ideas was August 18th, 1951. Veeck's St. Louis Browns were dismal. Attendance was down, and Veeck was about to give people reasons to come to the park—other than to see his team win. On this day in August, the Browns played a memorable doubleheader against the Detroit Tigers at Sportsman's Park in St. Louis.

During the American League's 50th anniversary celebration, which happened to coincide with the 50th anniversary of the Falstaff Brewing Company (the Browns' radio sponsor), Veeck surprised fans by putting a clown on the field, persuading pitcher Satchel Paige to play the drums in a jazz quartet, and paying a 26-year-old, three-feet-seven inch, 65-pound midget to jump out of a seven-foot birthday cake wearing a Browns uniform and slippers turned up at the ends, like those of an elf.

But Veeck was not done. In the bottom of the first inning of the second game, fans were once again surprised, this time by the announcement of the midget entering the game as a pinch-hitter! Over the public address system, the words rang out, "Number one-eighth, Eddie Gaedel, batting for Saucier."

Browns manager Zach Taylor sent Gaedel to the plate to pinch-hit. Tigers manager Red Rolfe immediately protested, but Taylor produced a legitimate contract, filed with the American League and cleared by umpire Ed Hurley.

Gaedel, whose strike zone measured 1.5 inches, drew a walk on four pitches from amused Tigers' pitcher Bob Cain. Then he ran to first base and was replaced by pinch-runner Jim Delsing. Gaedel received a standing ovation from Browns fans and promptly retired on the spot. His brief Major League career was over, just minutes after it had begun.

Fans were hoping to see Gaedel swing his toy-like bat— assuming Cain could get a pitch in his strike zone. But Gaedel was instructed by Veeck not to swing. The owner told his one-day wonder to crouch as low as possible, and warned him not to swing. Veeck even told Gaedel that, for good measure, a high-powered rifle would be trained upon him from the stands. Gaedel was happy to take a walk, and make history as the shortest baseball player ever to appear in a big-league game.

In the end, the Browns lost the game 6-2, despite the hoopla. For Gaedel's contribution, he was paid $100. Two days after the game, Gaedel, who had been insured by Veeck for $1 million, was banned from appearing in any more Major League games by American League president Will Harridge, who was so furious about Veeck's antics that he (unsuccessfully) tried to strike Gaedel's name from the baseball record books. But Veeck prevailed, making a mark on the game that would not be forgotten.

LOVE MATCH

F ormer Pittsburgh Pirates home-run
king Ralph Kiner was among the greatest
players of his era. He led the National League
in home runs seven consecutive seasons,
from 1946 to 1952, and was elected into
the Baseball Hall of Fame in 1975. But as a
baseball announcer, Kiner was known as the
master of malapropisms. In fact, his propensity for amazing
lines during broadcasts was so renowned that his verbal
missteps became known as "Kiner-isms." Among his most
classic Kinerisms were the following two:

"All of the Mets' road wins against the Dodgers this year
have been at Dodger Stadium."

"The Hall of Fame Ceremonies are on the 31st and 32nd
of June."

One day, during a break in a broadcast, Kiner was telling
his broadcasting buddy, Lindsey Nelson, about his wife, the
former tennis star Nancy Chaffee.

"When I married Nancy, I vowed I'd beat her at tennis
someday," Kiner told Nelson. "After six months, she beat me
6-2. After a year, she beat me 6-4. After we were married a year
and a half, I pushed her to 7-5. Then it happened: She had a
bad day, and I had a good one, and I beat her 17-15."

"Good for you, Ralph," exclaimed Nelson. "Was she sick?"

"Of course not!" Kiner snapped indignantly. "But she was
eight months pregnant."

BASEBALL'S ALL-RELIGION TEAM

C   Steve Christmas
1B   Jim Gentile
2B   Lave Cross
SS   Johnny Temple
3B   Max Bishop
OF   John Moses
OF   Angel Mangual
OF   Bob Christian
OF   Von Joshua
OF   Larry Parrish
OF   Luke Easter
OF   Johnny Priest
OF   Howie Nunn
OF   Billy Sunday
DH   Bris Lord
P   Eddie Solomon
P   Adrian Devine
P   Preacher Roe
P   Bill Parsons
P   Amos Russie
P   Micah Bowie

PAR FOR THE COURSE

F ormer President Bill Clinton was known as a golf lover throughout his two terms in the White House. But the way he played the game was always something of a question.

In May, 2000, Georgia Tech golfer Bryce Molder, ranked fourth in the NCAA at the time, was honored to play a round of golf with President Clinton at Chenal Country Club in Little Rock, Arkansas.

Molder's impression of the outing? "Playing with the president was weird," he remarked after the experience. "He shot a 90, but at the end of the game his scorecard said 84."

According to *New York Times* reporter Don Van Natta, the author of *First Off the Tee*, this was not unusual for Clinton, who once took some 200 swings to card an 82. Van Natta coined a term for Clinton's mulligans: "Billigans."

SAY WHAT?

"Every time we've lost, it's because we didn't score enough points."

RAY ALLEN
guard, Seattle Sonics

DID YOU KNOW?

 Did you know...that during his college career at LSU, "Pistol" Pete Maravich scored 50 or more points 28 times, and 40 or more points 56 times?

FORE SCORE

Gerald Ford, the 38th President of the United States, was an outstanding football player, but his athletic talent didn't follow him to the golf course. During his brief time in office, President Ford became known as one of the most dangerous golfers in America. It wasn't altogether uncommon for Ford to mistakenly hit a spectator with an errant tee shot.

One day, Ford was playing golf with Detroit Red Wings hockey legend Gordie Howe. On one hole, Howe offered to concede a simple two-foot putt to his distinguished opponent. Ford insisted on attempting the putt. He missed.

"We won't count that one," Howe generously told the president.

"Maybe you won't," Ford retorted as he gestured toward the assembled reporters standing on the edge of the green. "But they will!"

BULLETIN BOARD MATERIAL

Before taking his passing-game mastery to the NFL, Steve Spurrier became one of college football's most successful coaches while at the helm of the University of Florida. Under Spurrier, the Gators won a national title and were consistently among the country's top 10 teams.

Spurrier was known to rile his opponents on more than one occasion, via his inflammatory choice of words. Two of the old ball coach's most famous remarks came at the expense of vaunted rivals.

One year, during an off-season speaking tour to Gator booster clubs, Spurrier chose to take a poke at arch-rival Florida State. The Seminoles had recently learned that a Tallahasse shoe store had given members of the FSU team free shoes, which was a violation of NCAA rules. Spurrier couldn't resist the opportunity to rub it in a bit. He told Gator boosters how he was making plans for the coming season and had strategies in place to defeat FSU, or "Free Shoes University." As expected, the boosters roared with approval.

But perhaps Spurrier's most-famous comments came in discussing an upcoming game with sectional rival Auburn University. Spurrier informed Gator fans that, tragically, 20 books had been destroyed in a fire at Auburn's football dormitory.

"But the real tragedy," he declared, "was that fifteen hadn't been colored in yet!"

WHAT'S BREWING?

In 1972, the Milwaukee Brewers started their season in a terrible slump. They lost 20 of their first 30 games, essentially putting them out of playoff contention after completing just the first month on their schedule.

Needless to say, the team's struggles were wearing on Brewers manager Dave Bristol, who was quickly losing his sense of humor. After one loss during the span, Bristol laid down the law with his team.

"There'll be two buses leaving the hotel for the park tomorrow," he announced. "The two o'clock bus will be for those who need a little extra work. The empty bus will leave at five o'clock."

DID YOU KNOW?

Former teammates Fernando Valenzuela and Dave Stewart both threw no-hitters on the same day, June 30, 1990. Valenzuela's came for the Dodgers, Stewart's for the A's.

BASEBALL'S ALL-TERRAIN TEAM

Lineup Card

Team ___ALL TERRAIN___

Pos.	Player
C	STEVE LAKE
1B	DAVE VALLE
2B	GARY WOODS
SS	GENE ALLEY
3B	BROOK JACOBY
OF	MICKEY RIVERS
OF	TOM MARSH
OF	LOUIE MEADOWS
OF	RON STONE
DH	RUBEN SIERRA
PH	DUSTY RHODES
P	CHAN HO PARK
P	JOSE MESA
P	DOUG CREEK
P	LEE TUNNELL

GOING TO THE SOURCE

George Davis was a *Los Angeles Times* sportswriter during the first half of the 20th Century. He covered college football with zeal.

On New Year's Day in 1938, he was covering the Rose Bowl in Pasadena, California. During a key point in what became a historic game between Stanford and Notre Dame, Stanford superstar running back Ernie Nevers was about the cross the goal line for a go-ahead touchdown when he was stopped by Notre Dame All-American tackle Harry Stuhldreher. Stanford players, coaches, and fans felt Nevers had crossed the goal line prior to being hit by Stuhldreher and insisted Stanford had been robbed of a touchdown. For years thereafter, many Stanford fans remained steadfast that Notre Dame had stolen a victory.

One evening, Davis was arguing the point with some football fans at a restaurant, when a stranger interrupted and interjected his opinion. "I say he didn't score," the man declared.

"Where were you sitting?" Davis challenged. "I was sitting on Nevers's neck," the man replied. "I'm Harry Stuhldreher."

TEAMMATES

Rod Hundley was one of the NBA's most colorful characters, known more for his moves off the court than on. A Los Angeles Lakers guard who gained the nickname "Hot Rod," he once roomed with superstar Lakers forward Elgin Baylor, one of the greatest scorers in the history of the NBA.

One night in New York in 1971, Baylor set what was then a team record, scoring 71 points in a single game. As they got into a cab to ride back to their hotel, Hundley put an arm around his teammate and proudly proclaimed, "What a night we had, buddy! Seventy-three points between us!"

In one memorable high school game in 1937, all of Pat McGee's St. Peter's teammates fouled out of the game. McGee finished the game alone— and won!

THE PIED PIPER?

Sporting events have seen all types of strange ejections—players from the sidelines, coaches, grounds-crew members, even fans. But the stadium organist?

That's exactly what happened during a minor league baseball game at Jack Russell Stadium in Florida during the 1985 season. The Clearwater Phillies were locked in a tight game when the stadium organist intervened on the Phillies' behalf, and was kicked out of the stadium by the umpiring crew.

The organist, Wilbur Snapp, felt the umpires had made a bad call against the Phillies, and he decided to make his opinion known. He reacted to the call by playing the song "Three Blind Mice." The umpires, reacting to the not-so-subtle message, immediately ejected Snapp from the stadium.

Until 1859, baseball umpires sat behind home plate—in rocking chairs.

BASEBALL'S ALL-APPAREL TEAM

Lineup Card	
Team	ALL APPAREL TEAM
Pos.	**Player**
C	JESSE LEVIS
1B	CAP ANSON
2B	SHANE HALTER
SS	SPIKE OWEN
3B	CLETE BOYER
OF	BOOTS DAY
OF	TY CLINE
OF	SAM FROCK
OF	SOCKS SEYBOLD
DH	COTTON NASH
P	GARY BUCKELS
P	JIM COATES
P	DON HOOD
P	JIM CONVERSE
P	JIM BLUEJACKET
P	TEX JEANES

WHEN I WANT YOUR OPINION, I'LL ASK FOR IT!

Golfer Tommy Bolt was one of the finest pro golfers in the 1940s and '50s. He was well-known for his sweet swing and tempestuous attitude. So mercurial was his temper that it sometimes got the best of him. Attempting to enliven a golf clinic one day, Bolt asked his teenaged son to "show the nice folks what I taught you." His son excitedly grabbed a nine-iron and threw it into the sky.

During one tournament, the impatient Bolt found himself joined by a caddy who was known around golf circles for his constant talking during rounds.

Bolt would tolerate no chatter from the caddy, and let him know about it. Before he teed off to start the round, Bolt ordered the caddy not to speak at all during the entire day, unless Bolt asked him a question. Even then, the caddy was told he could answer only with a "yes" or "no."

On one hole, after an errant tee shot, Bolt found his ball lying next to a tree. Surveying his situation, Bolt saw that he would be required to hit the ball under a

branch and over a lake to get onto the green. He got down
on his knees and looked through the trees, sizing up the shot.
Then he turned to his caddy and asked him:

"What do you think? Five-iron?" asked Bolt.

"No, Mr. Bolt," the caddy said.

"What do you mean not a five-iron?" Bolt snarled.
"Watch this shot."

The caddy held firm. "No, Mr. Bolt."

Bolt hit the ball anyway, and hit it well, placing it within
a few feet of the pin. He then turned to his caddy and hand-
ed him the five-iron. "Now what do you think about that?"
he asked. "Go ahead, you can talk now."

"Mr. Bolt," replied the caddy, "that wasn't your ball."

A REAL LONG-SHOT

Until the rules were changed in 1952, golf balls had to remain where they landed, and players finding an opponent's ball in the way were required to loft their balls up in order to reach a hole. This was a key component for one of golf's most amazing stories.

Nearly 100 years ago, a female golfer was competing in the 1912 Shawnee Invitational for Ladies at Shawnee-on-Delaware. She took a huge swing at her ball and watched as it sailed majestically into the Binniekill River. But, amazingly, the ball remained floating atop the water, making it possible for the golfer to hit it.

She leapt into a boat and set off in hot pursuit. She came to the ball and stood up in the boat to whack at it. Numerous times the woman took a powerful swipe at the ball. She eventually made contact and sent the ball up onto a small beach—1.5 miles from where she had started the hole!

After jumping out of the boat, the woman prepared to tackle her next obstacle. A heavily wooded forest lay between her ball and the hole. She continued to hack away and finally put her ball in the cup—166 strokes later. That's 166 strokes, not for the entire 18-hole day, but for just the 130-yard, par 3, 16th hole.

SAY WHAT?

"Last Question."

YAO MING

Houston Rockets center when asked
to identify his favorite English words.

DID YOU KNOW?

In 1998, the Independent League Pacific
Suns traded pitcher Ken Krahenbuhl
to the Greenville (Mississippi)
Bluesmen for a player to be
named, cash and 10 pounds
of Mississippi catfish.

AN ICY RECEPTION:

The 1982 AFC Championship game will long be remembered for the frigid conditions that surrounded it. The San Diego Chargers were playing the Cincinnati Bengals for the right to go to the Super Bowl. The game took place in Cincinnati's Riverfront Stadium in mid-January, with temperatures near zero. As if that wasn't bad enough, a strong wind was blowing into the stadium, creating a wind-chill temperature of minus-59 degrees—an unofficial record low for a championship game.

The Bengals wanted to use the cold to their advantage against their warm-weather opponents. So, to gain a psychological edge, Cincinnati's offensive lineman played the game in short-sleeve jerseys.

"The thought of standing out there without sweatshirts on was horrible," said Bengals guard Dave Lapham. "But we decided that since the Chargers play in perpetual springtime, we might really do a number on their heads."

Seeing the Bengals bare their biceps in the freezing weather did seem to stun Chargers, as they watched Cincinnati's front five take the field for pre-game warm-ups. San Diego lost the game 27-7.

Thus, the Bengals headed to the Super Bowl—and the Chargers home to warmer weather.

NOT EXACTLY WHISTLING DIXIE

When the Ohio State Buckeyes won the college football national championship in 2003, Buckeye fans felt the team had been restored to its glory days of the 1950s, '60s, and '70s, when they were perpetual national-title contenders. In those earlier years, the Buckeyes and rival Michigan were clearly the class of the Big 10 conference, with one team or the other typically finding itself in January's Rose Bowl.

During its powerhouse days, Ohio State dominated one team in particular: the University of Illinois. In fact, the Fighting Illini became such a doormat for OSU that Buckeye fans affectionately referred to them as the "Friendly Illini." The nickname even caught on with Illinois faithful after a while.

So, when the two teams met in 1958, the Illini knew they needed to find a creative game plan to stop the Buckeyes and their All-American fullback, Bob White. Thus, in an effort to stop White, each time the OSU offense lined up to snap the ball, the entire Illini defensive unit began to whistle in unison. But this was not just any type of whistling. All 11 players whistled loudly, in effort to mimic the sound of the bobwhite quail. It was an attempt to use the sound of the bobwhite to stop Bob White. And it worked… sort of.

The Illini defense held White to just 35 yards rushing, well under his season average of 125 yards per game.

But alas, Illinois couldn't muster enough offense to match the defensive tactics, and fell short once again, losing 19-13.

DID YOU KNOW?

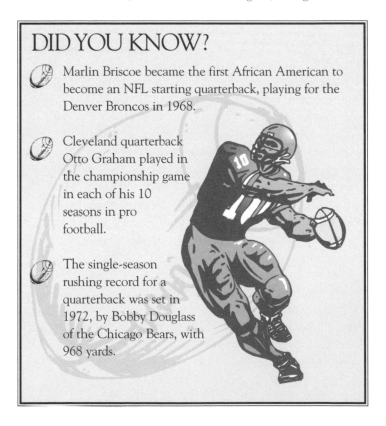

Marlin Briscoe became the first African American to become an NFL starting quarterback, playing for the Denver Broncos in 1968.

Cleveland quarterback Otto Graham played in the championship game in each of his 10 seasons in pro football.

The single-season rushing record for a quarterback was set in 1972, by Bobby Douglass of the Chicago Bears, with 968 yards.

ALL-THEOLOGY TEAM:

ART MONK
RICKY CHURCHMAN
LEMAR PARRISH
RANDY CROSS
JETHRO PUGH
HAVEN MOSES
ISAAC BRUCE
RICHARD BISHOP
PAUL BLESSING
DAVE CHAPPLE
BOBBY ABRAHAM
JEROME HEAVENS
STEVE LUKE
FREDDIE JOE NUNN
FRANK POPE
FREDDIE SOLOMON
RAY SERMON
SILAS TITUS

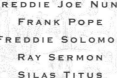

FAST TIMES IN THE MEDICAL PROFESSION

B ack in the 1970s, the international track and field world was stunned by the remarkable performance of a previously unheralded runner who blazed to sprint stardom in world competition.

Dr. Delano Meriwether was a unique talent—a flash-in-the-pan with a flashy personality to match. Rather than wearing the typical runner's shorts and tank top, Meriwether would step into the blocks for the 100-yard sprint wearing the wild combination of a hospital smock, suspenders, and a bathing suit—along with dark sunglasses.

The trademark get-up wasn't the only unusual thing about Meriwether. He was 28 years old, well beyond the age of most of the world's top sprinters. But beyond his age and his fashion tastes, Meriwether was a mystery. Rumor had it that he took up sprinting after his graduation from medical school in 1970. According to one story, he was watching a track meet on TV and turned to his wife after the 100-meter sprint was over. "I could beat those guys," he told her. Then he set about making good on his boast.

He practiced his starts in a Baltimore park at night, after finishing his duties as a hospital resident. "I never used a starter's gun," he explained once. "I didn't think it would be a very good idea for a black guy to be running fast in the park—and carrying a pistol."

At first, many track fans (and rivals) saw Meriwether as a sort of sideshow. They doubted that he could compete with other top runners, especially in his clownish outfit.

But complete and win Meriwether did. He won the 1971 AAU 100-yard dash—in a blistering nine seconds flat.

Five years later, Meriwether would be in the race of his life, or so he thought. In 1976, President Gerald Ford wanted a plan to tackle the dreaded swine flu epidemic. The task was put into the hands of a charismatic 33-year-old physician for the Department of Health, Education and Welfare. His name was Delano Meriwether, and he was still a world-class sprinter. Meriwether was given until the end of the year to get all 220 million Americans inoculated against swine flu. In the end, the threat never materialized and Meriwether remained known more for his exploits on the track than those in medicine.

DID YOU KNOW?

In his first game as baseball's first African American manager, Hall of Famer Frank Robinson inserted himself into the lineup, and homered to lead his Cleveland Indians to a 5-3 defeat of the Yankees on opening day, April 7, 1975.

BATTY PHILOSOPHY

N ew York Yankee great Yogi Berra has been beloved by baseball fans for more than 50 years. He embodies the innocence of the game and is perhaps the most-quoted sports figure of all time.

However, many people forget what a fine player Berra was. He was an all-star catcher and outfielder and a model for how to be a successful hitter.

A lifetime .285 batter with 358 home runs and 1,430 RBI to his credit, Berra was a 3-time American League MVP who played in 14 World Series. He was inducted into the Baseball Hall of Fame in 1972.

Berra's strategy at the plate was simple. "You can't hit and think at the same time," he once said.

Berra's philosophy was put to the test during his rookie season, when a veteran catcher tried to psych him out. As Berra stepped into the batter's box, the catcher informed him that the trademark label on his bat was turned the wrong way. (As a rule, batters want the trademark right-side-up when they hit.)

Berra, however, was unruffled. He turned to the catcher and said, "I didn't come up here to read." He then turned back to face the pitcher—and promptly hit the next pitch out of the ballpark for a home run.

BASEBALL'S ALL-FINANCIAL TEAM

REID NICHOLS

BARRY BONDS

OSCAR GAMBLE

ERNIE BANKS

CHUCK SCHILLING

DON MONEY

NORM CASH

FELIPE LIRA
WES STOCK
BRAD PENNY

JIM PRICE

 Mickey Mantle's salary in 1956, the year he won the Triple Crown, was $32,500.

MIND GAMES

Hall of Famer Carlton Fisk was known as one of the most talkative catchers in the game. He loved to talk to any batter, any umpire. He was always trying to use his yakking as a means to get a mental edge on a hitter.

Veteran umpire Ron Luciano recalls a time when Fisk got the better of a batter without saying one word to him. It was the conversation with Luciano, who was calling the game behind the plate that night, which created the distraction.

Fisk's Boston Red Sox were playing the Cleveland Indians during the summer of the 1976 season. The Indians sent up outfielder Charlie Spikes to pinch-hit late in the

Baseball Hall of Famer Rod Carew was born on a train.

game. As Spikes stepped into the batter's box, Fisk pretended to continue an ongoing conversation with Luciano.

"You're right, Ronnie, all he wants to do is throw that curveball," Fisk said, referring to his pitcher, Luis Tiant. Luciano had no idea what Fisk was talking about, so he did not respond.

Tiant's first pitch was a fastball for a strike, which Spikes watched as it whipped by him. Tiant's second pitch was a curveball that was outside for a ball. Fisk jumped up from behind the plate and trotted out to the mound, berating the pitcher. Returning to his spot, Fisk muttered to Luciano, "He says he misunderstood the sign."

Now, Luciano recognized that Fisk was setting up Spikes. He could tell Spikes was thinking hard about what was coming next, fastball or curve? Fisk gave Tiant signals for the next pitch, and the pitcher shook him off—which kept Fisk muttering to Luciano. Finally, the next pitch was a curveball that Spikes watched for strike two. Again, Fisk ran out to the mound, hollering at Tiant. As he came back this time, Fisk continued to engage Luciano, and Spikes. "He says that was a fastball. Now was that a fastball, Ronnie? Of course it wasn't."

At this point, Spikes was in mental knots, not knowing what was coming next. Tiant threw a fastball for strike three, with Spikes watching once again. During the entire time at the plate, Spikes had not even moved his bat.

DID YOU KNOW?

Babe Ruth once led the American League in earned-run average as a pitcher in 1916, going 23-13 with a 1.75 ERA

TRASH TALK

T im Wrightman was an All-American tight end at UCLA, who was drafted by the Chicago Bears in 1985. Wrightman, now an actor, remembers his rookie year in the National Football League, and how a wily veteran tried to get the best of him.

The Bears faced the Super Bowl-contending New York Giants, which meant Wrightman would spend much of the game lined up against superstar linebacker Lawrence Taylor. The rookie knew he would have his hands full attempting to block the fiercest pass rusher in the game. He studied film and carefully reviewed all of his assignments for each play. He wanted to be prepared for this enormous test of his ability to compete at the NFL level.

During his preparation, Wrightman learned about Taylor's infamous habit of talking to his opponents all game long, in an effort to wear them down emotionally. Few talked more trash than L.T., so Wrightman made sure he was ready for the verbal barrage.

Early in the game, Taylor looked Wrightman in the eyes and said, "Son, I'm going through you on the left; don't hurt yourself trying to stop me."

Wrightman, refusing to be intimidated, shot back, "Sir, is that your left or mine?"

The question froze Taylor long enough to allow Wrightman the chance to put a perfect block on him—and allow for a successful Bears offensive play.

Taylor was none too happy. He had been out-talked, by a rookie.

WORDS TO LIVE BY

"When I started to develop my fondness, or
my love, for athletics, it was because athletics
was a powerful way to influence youngsters
to be better people.... [The ultimate goal
of athletics] should be to help mold
young people to be our leaders."

TYRONE WILLINGHAM

head football coach, Notre Dame, who had an
83 percent graduation rate with Stanford.

YOU SCREAM, I SCREAM

I lie Nastase was known as one of the most enigmatic talents on the professional tennis tour. The Romanian was known as "Nasty" in tennis circles, which was by no means used as a term of endearment. Nastase was the originator of the over-the-top temper tantrum on the tennis court. Before there was McEnroe, there was Nasty.

However, Nastase was at the center of a humorous moment on the court, or perhaps better classified as a Good Humor moment.

At the 1973 Wimbledon tournament, Nastase was the number-one seed. This did not seem to make him any more serious than normal about his chances. At one point in the tournament, he pilfered an ice cream vendor's uniform, snuck into the crowd, and began to sell ice cream to the fans in attendance at center court.

One problem: At the refined All England Lawn and Tennis Club, where standards must be upheld, vendors are not allowed to sell their wares in the stands. Eventually, stewards approached Nastase and tossed him out of the stadium. When his identity was revealed, Nasty was mobbed by a pack of screaming local schoolgirls. He escaped the girls, and hid on the floorboards of a tournament official's car, and then made his way to safety.

Never again did Nastase attempt to sell ice cream at a match.

FACE THE MUSIC

Bill Veeck was an innovator and one of the most creative marketers the game of baseball has ever known. His promotional concepts are legendary. Not all of his ideas were good, however. Such is the case with "Disco Demolition Night," which he tried in 1979, while serving as general manager of the Chicago White Sox.

The event was conjured up by a Chicago-area disc jockey who despised disco music and wanted fans to make a statement about it being a bygone fad. The deal was that every fan who brought a disco record to the ballpark for a doubleheader with the Detroit Tigers on June 12 would be admitted for just 98 cents. Then, between games, all the albums would be burned on the field.

The disaster began during the first game, when LPs began flying like Frisbees onto the field in the middle of play. When the game finally ended, thousands of disco albums were exploded in a large container in center field. Unfortunately, this prompted hundreds of fans to storm onto the field, where they proceeded to pull up the bases, rip up patches of grass, and set fires to various items on the field.

After nearly an hour, and 37 arrests, order was restored. Surveying the scene, umpires ruled the field to be unplayable for the second game, and awarded the game, via forfeit, to the Tigers.

To his credit, Veeck later admitted his error in judgment, saying, "They came for the happening, and they won't come again. That was my biggest mistake."

AN OFFER HE COULDN'T REFUSE

Second baseman Steve Sax was a rookie sensation for the Los Angeles Dodgers in 1982. But the following season, he suddenly began to experience mysterious throwing problems. For some unknown reason, a toss to first base became a near impossibility. Some of Sax's throws sailed twenty or thirty feet over the first baseman's head—even when he was standing just 45 feet away. For the Dodgers that season, there was no such thing as a routine ground ball to second.

News of Sax's troubles spread around the league, and he became the object of much ridicule from opponents and fans. Opposing players seated in the first-base dugout would scurry out of the line of fire any time a ball was hit in the direction of Sax. Fans sitting behind first base held up signs that read, "Sax, throw me a souvenir."

The dumbfounded Sax spent hours of extra practice time working on his throws to first, and nearly each time he was right on target. He even practiced throwing to first while blindfolded, and had no trouble with accuracy. But during games, his wildness continued, signaling the issue was more mental than physical. For the season, Sax committed 30 errors, which easily led the league for his position. Twenty-eight of those errors came on throws.

Ever the optimist, Dodgers manager Tommy Lasorda attempted everything to help cure his second baseman and boost his confidence. "How many men are walking the streets of this great nation who can hit .280 in the Major Leagues like you're doing? Not many, right?" Lasorda would ask his young star.

"Right," Sax would reply.

"How many men out there can steal 50 bases in a season like you're doing? Not many, right?" the manager would continue.

"Right," Sax would again reply.

"Well, then," Lasorda would continue, "how many men can make a simple toss from second to first? Millions. In fact, there's ten million women who can do it! Right?"

Sax had to agree once again, but even Lasorda's lighthearted speeches didn't seem to make a difference.

Finally, Lasorda resorted to a practical joke that he and Dodgers bullpen coach Mark Crese pulled on Sax. One night during a road trip, Lasorda engaged Sax in a conversation while standing in a hotel lobby. While Sax's attention was diverted, Crese placed a large pig's head on a pillow under the sheets of the bed in Sax's hotel room. When Sax finally made it to his room that night, he was shocked to find the unexpected gift on his pillow. He was further worried when he read the note that accompanied it: "Saxy, you better start bearing down and throwing the ball right . . . or else. Signed, The Godfather."

As Sax told Lasorda of his finding, the prankster-manager fought to hold back his laughter, but lost control when Sax asked him in all seriousness, "Do you think the note might've been from a guy who lost money on a game because I threw a ball away?"

The laughter that ensued seemed to loosen Sax up, and perhaps contributed to him making great strides in overcoming his throwing problem. Over the final 38 games of the season, Sax made no errors.

BASEBALL'S ALL-ANATOMY TEAM

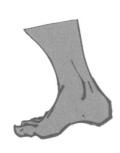

Pos.	Player
C	BARRY FOOTE
1B	HARRY CHEEK
2B	DAVE BRAIN
SS	GREG LEGG
3B	JIM HART
OF	BOB PATE
OF	MIKE PALM
OF	ED HEAD
P	BILL HANDS
P	RICH HAND
P	ROY FACE
P	ROLLIE FINGERS
P	RICKY BONES
P	BARTOLO COLON
P	MIKE OVERY
P	DON GULLETT
P	DAVE BEARD
P	SCOTT BROW

TRUE DEMOTION

Back in the late 1800s, during the earliest years of professional baseball, one of the game's very first stars was pitcher Joe Borden. Borden gave himself the nickname "Josephus the Phenomenal" because of his extraordinary pitching ability.

When the National League was founded in 1876, Borden was the winning pitcher in the very first game. He also pitched the first no-hitter. Boston Braves owner Nathaniel Apollonio decided to reward Borden for his achievements by giving him a three-year contract, in a day in which multiyear contracts were unheard of. His salary was $2,000 per year, which in that day was exorbitant.

When Borden failed to produce according to Apollonio's expectations, he was demoted to the position of groundskeeper to earn his huge salary. Soon, the owner became dissatisfied with Borden's work on the grounds, but had no other place to give him work. So, Boston bought out the remainder of his contract and sent him packing. At the tender age of 22, Josephus the Phenomenal was out of baseball for good.

Former Detroit Tigers outfielder Willie Horton was the youngest of 21 children.

HEAVYWEIGHT NEGOTIATOR

Charlie Kerfeld broke into the Major Leagues with an impressive rookie season in 1986. The relief pitcher posted a record of 11-2 with a 2.59 ERA and seven saves. When he renegotiated his contract with the Houston Astros for the 1987 season, Kerfeld had some rather odd demands in order to close the deal.

The right-handed relief pitcher was fond of his uniform number 37 and wanted to find a way to memorialize it in his contract. So when the Astros offered him a salary of $110,000 for the season, Kerfeld turned it down, insisting the team pay him $110,037.37. He further demanded the team throw in 37 boxes of Jell-O to complete the agreement. The Astros said yes to both the additional $37.37, and the 37 boxes of Jell-O, and Kerfeld was happy.

He was not thin, however, and within two years, weight problems drove him out of the game at age 24. When Kerfeld was released, many wondered what would have happened had he not insisted on the Jell-O.

Immediately after recording his 3000th hit on September 30, 1992, Hall of Famer George Brett was picked off first base by Angels pitcher Tim Fortugno.

SHORT STOP?

Bill Sharman was a part of one of the finest backcourt tandems in NBA history. In the 1950s, Sharman teamed with Bob Cousy to help lead the Boston Celtics to four NBA championships. One of the greatest free throw shooters ever, Sharman hit 88.3% of his shots from the charity stripe over his career and led the league in free throw percentage a record seven times. He was elected to the Pro Basketball Hall of Fame in 1975. Sharman also coached the Los Angeles Lakers to an NBA title in 1972, a season in which his team won a league record 33 consecutive games.

What most people don't remember about Sharman, is that he also played baseball, making it to the Major Leagues. But his stay in the big leagues was one of the shortest and oddest ever known.

Late in the 1951 season, the Brooklyn Dodgers called Sharman up to be with the team during the pennant race. Sharman rode the bench as the Dodgers blew a huge lead in the final month, and never got into a game. During a game on September 27, the Dodgers were involved in a tense battle, and emotions were a bit raw. Several players took exception to some calls made by umpire Frank Dascoli and began to make their displeasure known from the bench.

Dascoli was not happy. After a warning to the Dodgers bench, the razzing continued, so Dascoli decided to throw the entire Brooklyn bench out of the game. Every player, including Sharman, was ordered to leave the dugout. Thus, Bill Sharman became the only player in baseball history to be thrown out of a Major League game without having played in one.

BETTER THAN WHEATIES

Doug Rader was one of the National League's premier third basemen in the late 1960s and early '70s. Most of his playing career was spent with the Houston Astros. Later, Rader managed the Texas Rangers, California Angels, and Chicago White Sox. During his playing days, he was known as a solid power hitter who also had a good glove. He hit 20 or more homers three times and drove in 80 or more runs four times during in a five-year stretch, while leading the NL's third basemen in fielding percentage and assists twice each.

But Rader was also quirky, and known for occasional wacky behavior. Often, teammates would catch him eating baseball cards in the dugout during games. When they asked him why he was munching on the cardboard, Rader replied by saying it was the best and quickest way that he could absorb statistical information of the opposing players.

ALL-FOOTBALL APROPOS NAME TEAM

Pos.	Player
LB	TRAVIS HITT
DT	JERRY BALL
RB	JIM KIICK
QB	BOB BOUNDS
LB	JOHN HUDDLESTON
LB	DOAK FIELD
RB	LARRY CENTERS
TE	MIKE FLAGG
RB	DICKIE POST
DE	ROD CURL
QB	WILLIE THROWER
DB	MICHAEL DOWNS
DB	MIKE HOLDER
DE	STEVE BAACK
P	SCOTT PLAYER

HEAD BANGER

During a nationally televised Monday Night Football game, the game's most devastating blow was delivered by none other than a quarterback. Unfortunately, he was also the recipient of that blow.

In 1997, Gus Frerotte was quarterbacking the Washington Redskins as they took on the New York Giants. The 'Skins were underdogs and their offense, with Frerotte at the helm, had come under fire from the media in recent weeks.

With 2:16 left in the first half, Frerotte went back to pass. A good push from the defensive line forced Frerotte to scramble out of the pocket. After escaping Giants defensive end Bernard Holsey, he found an open lane to the goal line, and sprinted into the end zone to give the Redskins a 7-0 lead.

Frerotte was so excited about scoring that he celebrated by firing the football at the wall behind the end zone. Not yet done, Frerotte lowered his helmet and head-butted the wall. Unfortunately the wall was immobile, and Frerotte got the worst of the encounter. He recoiled in pain, fell to the ground, and signaled for immediate medical attention from the sideline.

After being treated, Frerotte returned for one series at the end of the half, then didn't return from the locker room at halftime. He was taken to a hospital for examination, then later returned to the stadium, where he watched the remainder of the game from the locker room.

As the national TV audience endured what would end in a 7-7 tie, they learned that Frerotte had knocked himself out of the game and sustained a concussion that would sideline him for a few weeks. It was clearly one of the NFL's more embarrassing moments.

"It was stupid, but I was fired up," Frerotte said of his escapade. "Things weren't going well, then I get a big play like that."

Redskins head coach Norv Turner said wryly following the game: "I never thought to tell a guy not to do that."

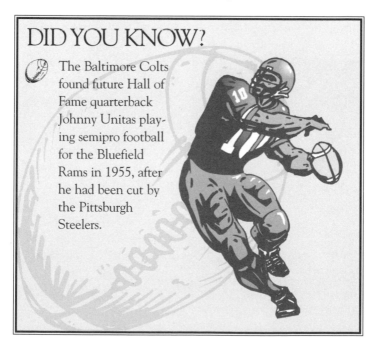

DID YOU KNOW?

The Baltimore Colts found future Hall of Fame quarterback Johnny Unitas playing semipro football for the Bluefield Rams in 1955, after he had been cut by the Pittsburgh Steelers.

THE DAY THE SCOUTS SLEPT IN

In 1946, the Washington Redskins used their number-one pick in the NFL draft to select back Cal Rossi out of UCLA. Unfortunately, Redskins officials failed to realize that Rossi had only completed his junior year and was thus ineligible to be drafted.

But the Redskins were determined to get their man, so they waited until the next year, hoping to draft Rossi again. In 1947, when the 'Skins first-round choice came up, they chose Rossi a second time. Once again, team officials must not have done their homework, because Rossi had declared that he had no intention of playing professional football.

When Rossi lived up to his vow, the Redskins were deprived of their top pick for the second year in a row—setting a yet-unequalled level of NFL draft incompetence.

The 1972 Miami Dolphins became the first team in history to have two thousand-yard rushers on the same team—Larry Csonka and Mercury Morris.

ET TU, BUTKUS

Dick Butkus was one of pro football's greatest defensive players. With a fierce disposition on the field, he struck fear in the hearts of opponents. Butkus played up his persona off the field as well. His running through walls and other exploits helped draw a picture of a man who was a bit crazy. The Chicago Bears Hall of Fame linebacker liked it that way, because it meant running backs had a second thought when they came his way with ball in hand.

That is why many thought it odd when, in 1969, Butkus became interested in Shakespeare. A friend had told Butkus that he should study Shakespeare because it would help him with his public speaking skills, which could help land more off-field opportunities.

"Some people think I have to get down on all fours to eat my four pounds of raw meat every day," Butkus told the astonished press corps about his new-found interest. "But people who know me know that I can read. I move my lips a little,

but I can read things of a second-grade level—like newspapers
—and I don't really need a rubber stamp to give my auto-
graph."

Butkus also told the media that he felt he could apply
the wisdom of Shakespeare on the field. When asked how,
he explained. "Take this situation: One of our men is shaken
up on a play and is slow getting up. The opposing blocker is
standing over him laughing, as often happens during a game. I
walk over there and instead of swearing and snarling at the guy,
maybe getting thrown out of the game, I just tell him, 'He jests
at scars that never felt a wound.' Now that is bound to set him
thinking and teach him a little humility."

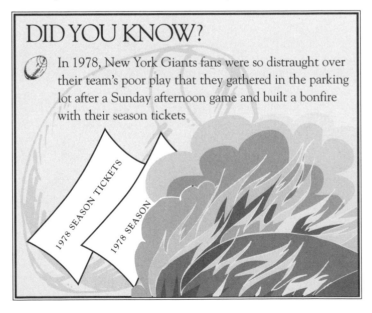

DID YOU KNOW?

In 1978, New York Giants fans were so distraught over
their team's poor play that they gathered in the parking
lot after a Sunday afternoon game and built a bonfire
with their season tickets

PLAYING CHICKEN

Typically when a basketball game is out of reach late in the contest, most fans head for the exits to beat the traffic and get an early start toward home. Unless, that is, they have something to stick around for.

Playing in their home opener in 1978, the Houston Rockets led the New York Knicks by 40 points in the fourth quarter. The game was clearly out of reach, but nearly every Rockets fan stayed to the very end. That's because each basket Houston scored brought the fans a step closer to a special prize—a free chicken dinner courtesy of a local fast-food chain.

The promotional offer made by Ron Krispy Fried Chicken was a free chicken dinner for every ticket holder attending a game in which the Rockets scored 135 points or more—a total the team had reached just once in its eight-year history. The chain felt good about the offer, thinking the chances of the team reaching that mark were slim.

But midway through the final period, the crowd was reminded of the offer by the public address announcer. The fans began to chant, "We want chicken! We want chicken!" The players were not about to leave their fans disappointed, so they quickened the pace of the game and began to make a run at the magic number. Rockets coach Tom Nissalke got into it, too, and sent his starters back into the game. With that move, the fans changed their chant to "Tom wants chicken! Tom wants chicken!"

With 51 seconds remaining in the game, and Houston leading 133-83, Mike Dunleavy drove to the hoop and made a lay-up, sending the crowd into a state of pandemonium.

The next day, 4,000 fans showed up at Ron Krispy outlets around the Houston area and redeemed their ticket stubs. The happy fans made quick work of more than $6,000 worth of chicken and, for a second consecutive night, went home happy.

For his efforts, Dunleavy was presented with a new nickname by his teammates: Chicken Man.

WHERE HAVE YOU GONE, BILL VEECK?

During his years as general manager of the Philadelphia 76ers, Pat Williams gained a reputation as a shrewd and some-times risky promoter. His team had the great Julius Erving, which gave fans ample reasons to come watch the team. But Williams was willing to try some other methods to create hype around his team and to put more people into the seats. Many of his ideas worked. Others were a bit like sideshow gimmicks. For Williams, it really didn't matter, as long as the fans enjoyed themselves. "My philosophy is for the fans to have fun," he once said. More often than not, they did.

His most notable events included Blind Date Night, in which willing male participants were given odd-numbered seats and willing female participants even-numbered seats next to the men. The evening then became a blind date for the couples seated next to each other. The good news—56 eager men showed up to take part. The bad news—only four women joined them.

Williams also tried a promotion in which fans were challenged to grapple with Victor the Wrestling Bear in between games of a rare basketball doubleheader. The stunt fizzled when participants realized that Victor was toothless and had been declawed.

When the wrestling bear didn't work, Williams tried to

make a special night out of the performance of Little Arlene, a 105-pound youth who wolfed down 77 hot dogs, 21 pizzas, and 19 sodas as amazed fans looked on in disbelief.

Then there was the promotion involving Chick the Singing Pig. The swine came out at halftime to sing for the crowd, but while in the spotlight at center court, managed only an off-key oink before relieving himself on the floor. The fans would not let this one pass without making their disapproval known. A newspaper headline the next morning read: KNICKS WHIP 76ERS, PIG BOOED.

"What did they expect," asked Williams, "Grand Opera?"

ALL MUSICAL TEAM:

G- RAJA BELL

G- RON HORN

C- BERNARD TOONE

F- JOHN BACH

F- RUDY KEYS

DEE-FENSE!

One of the most amazing basketball games of all time must also have been the most difficult to watch.

In 1925, Kensal High and Pingree High, two Fargo, North Dakota, girls high school teams were locked in a defensive struggle. They played to a scoreless tie at the end of regulation time.

After three overtime periods, the teams were still deadlocked at 0-0. It was determined that the best solution was to keep the girls from taking the court again and decide the contest by flipping a coin. While the referee flipped a quarter, Kensal's weary coach correctly called heads, and Pingree wound up a 0-0 loser.

YOU WIN SOME,
YOU LOSE SOME

The most famous coin toss in basketball history was one that took place with the principals participating via telephone, and the fortunes of one franchise dramatically changed by the side on which the coin landed.

In the 1960s, the NBA decided to determine the team that would hold the first pick in the college player draft by the flip of a coin. The two teams with the worst records would be involved in the coin toss, with the team winning the toss receiving the first pick.

At no time was the toss of the coin more important than in 1969. The Phoenix Suns and the Milwaukee Bucks had the league's worst records during the regular season. Each was in need of a franchise savior and dreamed about the possibility of obtaining UCLA graduate Lew Alcindor (later to become Kareem Abdul-Jabbar), who many basketball experts regarded

as the greatest
college player
ever. Whichever
team won the
toss would
become
an instant
championship
contender—and
a magnet for
national media
coverage, endorse-
ments, and the like.

Executives from both
teams were connected by
telephone from their home offices
to the NBA headquarters in New York. NBA
Commissioner Larry Kennedy was on the phone to oversee the
proceedings. The Suns, by virtue of having the worst record,
made the call. As Kennedy announced to all listening that he
was tossing the coin in the air, Suns General Manager Jerry
Colangelo made the call: Tails. The coin came up heads, and
the Suns' misfortune became the Bucks gold mine. Within one
year, Alcindor led Milwaukee to a league championship and
was named the NBA's MVP.

The Suns? With the second pick, they selected 6-10
center Neal Walk from Florida. Walk had a modest career in
Phoenix, but the difference between him and Jabbar was as
profound as the difference between heads and tails.

DOUBLE WHAMMY

In 1912, boxing fans witnessed one of the most perplexing outcomes in the sport's history.

The record book shows that Ad Wolgast defended his lightweight title by knocking out "Mexican Joe" Rivers in the 13th round in an Independence Day bout held in Vernon, California, July 4th. What the record book does not indicate is that Wolgast was simultaneously knocked out by Rivers.

Yes, it was a double-knockout, the only one known to occur in a title fight in boxing history. Both fighters landed right-hand blows to the jaw, resulting in both men dropping unconscious—in unison—to the canvas.

Referee Jack Welch propped up Wolgast and proceeded to count out Rivers.

The crowd nearly rioted at the decision until Welch explained his questionable reason for favoring the champ: "He fell last."

YOU CAN'T WIN THEM ALL

Legendary Eddie Arcaro is the only jockey in horse racing history to have won five Kentucky Derbies, six Preakness Stakes, and six Belmont Stakes. He also won more than 5,000 races in his long and illustrious career. But the way he started his foray into riding horses gave no indication as to what was ahead.

Some were wondering if Arcaro had what it took to be a successful jockey when they watched him lose the first 250 consecutive races of his career.

But even Arcaro was better than Juan Vinales, who became something of a folk hero at the track for his string of losses. The Puerto Rican jockey retired in 1961, at the age of 28, with a record that most horse racing analysts believe will never be broken. In 360 career mounts, Vinales never won a race.

NOW YOU SEE IT; NOW YOU DON'T

Dave Hampton was a fine NFL running back for the Green Bay Packers and Atlanta Falcons. He had a solid career; however, it was marked by one of the most unfortunate individual moments for any player.

One thousand yards rushing in a single season is the benchmark for all great running backs. It's an elite club that all ball carriers strive to join.

In the 1972 season, Hampton had an opportunity to reach that milestone in the Falcons season finale against the Kansas City Chiefs. Late in the fourth quarter, a six-yard run put Hampton over the 1,000-yard mark. The game was temporarily stopped, while Hampton was presented the game ball in a brief ceremony, during which Falcons fans cheered wildly for their first 1,000-yard rusher in franchise history.

To the dismay of the fans, and especially Hampton, his achievement lasted but a few moments. A few plays later, Hampton took a handoff and was dropped for a six-yard loss. Game circumstances led to Hampton getting the ball just one more time, on a play that netted just a one-yard gain. As the clock ran out on the game, and the Falcons season, Hampton was left with the empty feeling that he had been a 1,000-yard rusher for only a brief time. The season ended with Hampton totaling 995 yards.

QUICK THINKING?

Harry Wismer was one of the most famous sports announcers of the early days of sports radio. Known as Hairbreadth Harry, Wismer was renowned for his knack for never missing a beat when calling a play—even if it meant he had to make up some of the details. Since sports were not televised in those days, Wismer had the advantage of knowing that his listeners could not see the events unfolding before their eyes. This was helpful when Wismer became confused or made an incorrect call, as he could simply find his way out through creative announcing. At times, Wismer was able to describe a play any way he wanted, and as long as he made it sound convincing, it didn't matter to his listeners.

In a famous Army football game in the early 1940s, Wismer was calling the exploits of Army's great running back tandem of Glenn Davis and Doc Blanchard. On one play, Blanchard took a handoff and raced 75 yards for a touchdown. Wismer, however, mistakenly thought the ball had been given to Davis, and he began to call the play as such. Wismer was excitedly describing Davis's running toward the end zone, noting that the All-American made it to the 10-yard line. Only then did Wismer realize that it was not Davis but Blanchard who actually had the ball. He simply adjusted in mid-sentence to correct his call: "He's at the twenty…the ten…and Glenn laterals to Blanchard—touchdown, Blanchard!"

IN THE TRADITION OF WISMER

C lem McCarthy was a well-liked radio announcer for horse races during the 1940s. He had his share of embarrassing moments on air, but none was quite like his call of the 1947 Preakness Stakes on a national radio network.

Here is how he called the race:

"This is going to be an awful horse race down here, but On Trust is still there. Jet Pilot is coming at him . . . Jet Pilot a half a length—Jet Pilot a length. On Trust second by three; Phalanx is third, and in fourth place—ladies and gentlemen, I've made a terrific mistake. I've mixed my horses, and I've given you the winner as Jet Pilot, and it is Faultless. Just at what point I was looking at Phalanx and Jet Pilot disappeared on me, I don't know. The winner of the race is Faultless. All right, we missed; we struck out. Well Babe Ruth struck out once, so I might as well get in famous company."

When asked later about his colossal blunder, McCarthy explained that the crowd had blocked his view at the exact moment that Faultless moved into Jet Pilot's position. Later, noted sports filmmaker Bud Greenspan showed film footage to verify McCarthy's story. Prior to Greenspan's revelation, however, no one in racing circles accepted the explanation. When he was asked how he wound up calling the wrong winner, McCarthy cryptically referred to Wismer's infamous methods of making stuff up on the fly, saying, "You can't lateral to a horse."

THE HEIDI BOWL

There are numerous sports broadcasting blunders on record, but perhaps none is quite as notorious as NBC's telecast of the AFL game between the New York Jets and Oakland Raiders on November 17, 1968.

The game, which was played in Oakland, had significant consequences for the AFL playoffs. The Raiders were chasing the Kansas City Chiefs for the Western Division title, and the Jets were also trying to secure a playoff berth in the East. Kansas City had already won its game that day, so the eyes of the football world were fixed on this game.

It was a big ratings day for NBC, which had already scheduled the family film *Heidi* as a special Sunday night movie. The movie was to follow the game at 7 p.m. in all of the United States, except the West Coast, which was on a three-hour delay. The NBC Network control had instructions to run *Heidi* as scheduled, unless they received a phone call from a network executive telling them to delay the start of the movie to accommodate the completion of the game, should the game run long.

At approximately 6:50 p.m., the game was tied 29-29. Don Ellis, the NBC producer in the television truck on-site in Oakland, warned West Coast Network Control that the game might go past 7 p.m. Eastern time and asked them what Network Control in New York was going to do. At the same time, a number of East Coast viewers who were avid Jets fans began to ask themselves the same question. They had heard promotional announcements throughout the game about the movie starting at 7, and now, with the clock ticking ominously toward that hour—and the game's outcome in doubt—these viewers wondered what NBC was going to do. So they began to call the network offices in New York. There were so many calls, in fact, that the NBC switchboard blew a fuse.

NBC executives Chet Simmons and Julian Goodman were each watching the game at home and realized that they better keep the game on the air and delay the start of *Heidi*. But when the two men attempted to call to Network Control, they received a constant busy signal. With the switchboard out, they could not get through. They also tried the Network Control hotline, which was set up for emergencies like this, but that line had been disconnected a short time earlier because too many employees had been using it to make personal long-distance calls. The network executives could not call in, and the network control technicians could not call out. NBC had a serious problem.

At about 6:58 p.m., Jim Turner of the Jets kicked a field goal to put New York ahead 32-29 with 1:05 remaining in the game. The producer, Ellis, was now in a panic. He couldn't believe the network was actually going to switch over to *Heidi*, and he couldn't reach Simmons to discuss the situation. Every time he tried to call Simmons, he got a busy signal. This, of course, was because Simmons was on the phone trying to get through to the switchboard so he could reach Ellis. The result was a constant busy signal for both men. At 6:59, one executive got through to the NBC affiliate in Oakland and was able to relay a message to Ellis to tell West Coast Control to tell

New York Control not to switch over to the movie. But by the time word got through to New York, the network-control technicians thought Ellis was just making it up in an attempt to keep his game on the air. Since the command did not come from an executive, the technicians did not believe Ellis.

At 7 p.m., just as Turner's kickoff fell into the arms of Raider kick returner Charlie Smith, *Heidi* came on televisions across America, except for on the West Coast. Within a few minutes, the Raiders offense marched downfield, scored, and won the game.

New York fans were outraged. Many could not learn until the next day that the Jets had lost. Those who watched the Sunday night news did get a report on the game, however. It included this from a local sportscaster: "Jets thirty-two, Oakland forty-three . . . and Heidi married the goatherd."

WHO WAS THAT MASKED MAN?

One of the sporting world's most infamous figures has worn many athletic uniforms but never participated in a single game.

Barry Bremen is the ultimate sports gate crasher. In the 1970s and '80s, he routinely made appearances, posing as an athlete, at major sporting events.

At the 1979 NBA All-Star game, the 32-year-old old insurance salesman from Detroit temporarily eluded security guards and showed up on the court in a makeshift uniform. He mixed in with the players during warm-ups, and even made a lay-up while taking part in pre-game drills with the real all-stars before he was caught. Bremen did it all on a dare and a $300 bet.

He was quickly in the news, invited to appear as a guest on *The Today Show* and *The Tonight Show*. Perhaps inspired by his newfound fame, Bremen decided to expand his impersonation gig. Within a year of his first feat, he played a practice round of golf at the U.S. Open, shagged fly balls in the outfield with players before the baseball All-Star game, sat on the bench in full uniform at the NFL Pro Bowl in Hawaii, and came onto the ice as a referee at the NHL All-Star game.

For his ultimate stunt, Bremen went all out. He targeted Texas Stadium and the Dallas Cowboys. Bremen's goal was to make it onto the field for a game, in full uniform. However, his aim was to do it not as a Dallas Cowboy, but rather as a Dallas Cowboy cheerleader. So, there he was, complete with makeup, wig, hot pants, white boots, halter top and false enhancements, running onto the field with the rest of the Cowboys' famed cheerleaders. He made a quick romp in front of the television cameras and sputtered a squeaky falsetto "Go Cowboys!" before the gig was up. Within a few minutes, Bremen was handcuffed and arrested for trespassing.

The Cowboys organization did not find Bremen's antics amusing. They wanted him prosecuted, ordered to pay $10,000 in damages and have him banned for life from Texas Stadium. Bremen was amazed, saying, "I'm not really kinky. I was just having fun."

DID YOU KNOW?

In 1962, the Buffalo Bills claimed a San Diego Chargers quarterback on waivers, for $100, to become their starter. This man later led the Bills to AFL championship wins over the Chargers in 1964 and '65. His name: Jack Kemp.

HAVE A NICE STAY

M ost aspiring baseball players dream about the first day they make it to the big leagues. "What would it feel like to put on the uniform and run out onto a Major League field?" they wonder

For Harry Heitman, the dream didn't match reality. On July 27, 1918, Heitman joined the Brooklyn Dodgers. On that first day, he was to pitch against the St Louis Cardinals. He had hardly warmed up when his dream came crashing down. Heitman faced just five batters, getting only one out.

The other four hitters he faced ripped two triples and two singles, before Heitman was removed from the game.

He walked off the mound to the showers with an ERA of 108.00, and he just kept walking, never to return. That very afternoon, Heitman tossed his glove in the trash and enlisted in the Navy.

IT WAS A GREAT MOMENT, BUT I DON'T REMEMBER MUCH

B illy Herman was a fine Major League player during the 1930s. The Chicago Cub second baseman played for nearly two decades, made several All-Star teams, and had a lifetime .304 batting average. But the beginning of Herman's career was not exactly memorable—at least for him.

For his big-league debut, Herman was in the starting lineup against the Cincinnati Reds and pitcher Si Johnson. Eager to prove he belonged, Herman dug into the batter's box with steely determination. At Johnson's first pitch, Herman swung so hard that when he foul-tipped the ball, it hurtled the ground in back of home plate with such spin on it that the reverse English caused the ball to bounce straight back up into Herman's head. The force of the impact knocked him out cold.

Herman had to be carried off the field on a stretcher. In a rather ignominious beginning to what would turn out to be a great career, Billy Herman had knocked himself right out of the game, literally.

Ken Griffey Jr. and Stan Musial not only hail from the same birthplace, Donora, PA, but they also share the same birthday, November 21.

WHAT A CARD!

Many players have attempted to play pranks on the various sports trading-card companies. Each year, when the card companies send photographers to take pictures of the players, some attempt to sneak something into the shot to have their prank recorded for history. Some attempts actually make it past photographers and editors and wind up on the cards that are distributed to kids across America.

Such was the case in 1969 with a young third baseman named Aurelio Rodriguez.

When a photographer from the Topps trading-card company visited the California Angels to snap Rodriguez's picture, his teammates urged him to trick the photographer by switching uniforms with another player. Rodriguez agreed, and the Topps man, not knowing what the real Rodriguez looked like, shot the wrong person.

Thus, when Aurelio Rodriguez's 1969 Topps trading card #653 was released, it bore the baby-faced countenance of a 16-year-old Angels batboy named Leonard Garcia.

EXCUSES, EXCUSES

Many a player has attempted to come up with an excuse for sitting out a game in order to take a day off. Two of the more creative excuses around baseball circles still are talked about today.

Jose Cardenal was an outfielder for eight teams from 1963 to 1980. He was a decent player, but was reputed to be sometimes wanting out of the lineup. Cardenal was described as a player who felt if he couldn't give 100-percent effort, it would be better to give no effort at all. Many managers complained that they sometimes endured the difficult chore of arguing with Cardenal while he explained to them why he should remain in the comfort of the dugout rather than in the hot sun in right field.

During his time with the Chicago Cubs, one of Cardenal's managers was Whitey Lockman. Before one road game in 1972, Cardenal approached Lockman and told the manager he needed to sit out the game. When Lockman asked why, Cardenal's reply was "Crickets."

The manager told his player he needed more explanation. Cardenal replied by telling Lockman that the crickets in his hotel room the night before had made so much noise that he couldn't get to sleep and was too tired to play.

In 1974, Cardenal may have topped that explanation when he asked for a couple of days to sit out because his eyelid was stuck open.

EXCUSES, EXCUSES II

Perhaps it had something to do with playing outfield for the Cubs, but Chicago had another interesting "excuse" case before Cardenal.

Lou Novikoff played outfield for the Cubs from 1941 to 1944. His nickname was "The Mad Russian," but the moniker had little to do with his ethnic heritage.

Any time a ball was hit over his head in Chicago's Wrigley Field, Novikoff would back up only so far and then go no farther, no matter how far the ball was hit. Most often, the ball would carom off the wall and shoot past him, back toward the infield.

When frustrated Cubs manager Charlie Grimm asked Novikoff why he constantly gave up on the seemingly catchable balls, Novikoff explained that he had a terrorizing fear of vines. This was a real problem because all Cubs home games were played at Wrigley Field, whose walls are covered by ivy.

Grimm tried everything possible to cure his odd outfielder's fear. He brought in poisonous goldenrod to show Novikoff that the vines in Wrigley were not goldenrod. He even tried rubbing the Wrigley vines all over his own face and hands, and then chewed on them to prove the ivy was not poisonous. But Novikoff never was able to overcome his fear, and many balls continued to sail over his head.

SAY WHAT?

"I love third base. It's four steps to the dugout."

DMITRI YOUNG

Detroit Tigers, on being moved from 1st base to 3rd base in 2003.

DID YOU KNOW?

 Outfielder Chad Curtis was married to his wife, Candace, on May 7, 1990, at the courthouse in Davenport, Iowa, while wearing his Quad Cities Angels uniform, at 1:30 p.m. prior to his 2:00 p.m. minor league game.

A COSTLY SHOT

Earl Monroe was known during his NBA days as "Earl the Pearl." As he worked his magic for the Baltimore Bullets and New York Knicks in the 1960s and '70s, he exhibited style and flash that were rare for the era.

But Monroe's theatrics, which so often endeared him to fans, once left them sorely disappointed.

In 1977, Monroe's Knicks were leading the Portland Trail Blazers 108-102, with just two seconds remaining in the contest. With the Knicks controlling the ball after a timeout, all that remained was for New York to inbound the ball and let the final two ticks run off the clock. But Monroe had other ideas. He took the inbounds pass, eluded two defenders, then lofted a shot at the Blazers' basket. No one really knows what Monroe was thinking. Some speculated that he thought the clock had already run out. Others said it was the Pearl merely living up to his billing. Either way, the ball swished through the net just before the buzzer sounded. Two points were awarded to the Blazers.

While the Knicks still won the game, the final score was 108-104, rather than 108-102. To New York fans who had wagered on the game, this was a disaster. The betting line on the game had ranged from five-and-one-

half to seven points. So, all those who bet on the Knicks—
on the hopes of the team covering a spread of minus five-and-
a-half or six—had their winnings secure, until Monroe's final
act of showmanship. With the final score just a four-point
victory, all these bettors lost.

Because of the controversy over gambling scandals in
basketball, Monroe's actions came under intense scrutiny and
led to an inquiry by NBA officials. Ultimately, the league was
convinced that Monroe's shot was just the Pearl showing off,
rather than his participation in any type of gambling scheme.

Said Monroe, "I just threw the ball up and it went in—
the wrong place."

ALL VICE TEAM:

G- KENNY GAMBLE

G- LARRY STEELE

C- BOB BOOZER

F- RAY OWES

F- CLINT WAGER

THE DEFENSE RESTS

The Portland Trail Blazers were at the center of another unusual on-court occurrence that had NBA officials shaking their heads. In 1983, the Blazers were thrashing the Denver Nuggets. Late in the fourth quarter, the Blazers led 146-111. Flamboyant Denver coach Doug Moe, incensed at his team's lack of defensive showing throughout the game, learned that the Portland franchise's single-game scoring record was 150 points and came up with an unorthodox plan.

Moe called timeout and instructed his players to give the ball to the Blazers, and then not defend them at all. Moe reasoned that if Portland reached a new franchise record for points in a game, the new record would make that night's highlight reels and the next day's front-page headlines. He assumed his own team would be humiliated by the reports of their poor defensive showing, which would motivate them to improve.

Moe's players carried out the plan as their coach instructed. The Blazers broke the record, totaling 156 points, and the Denver players were humiliated. But the league officials weren't laughing. The strange ending sparked rumors that the game was "fixed." So, they slapped a $5,000 fine on Moe, along with an official reprimand.

Moe was outraged, but frank in his assessment of the evening's events, and the punishment he faced. "What makes the final minute any different from the defense we put up against them in the first and second quarters?" he asked rhetorically. "We didn't guard against them all night long."

ALL NAVY TEAM:

G- DARRELL CARRIER

G- JOHN BATTLE

C- CHARLIE SHIPP

F- TERRY FURLOW

F- KENNY SAILORS

ALL BOATING TEAM:

G- DANNY FERRY

G- MATT FINN

C- EDDIE MAST

F- CURTIS ROWE

F- LOUIS ORR

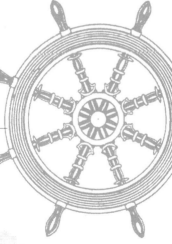

A NOT-SO-SUPER PASS

The most famous pass in Super Bowl history is not a game-winning touchdown strike from Joe Montana to Jerry Rice, or from the hand of Kurt Warner to Isaac Bruce. Nor is it a long spiral from Bart Starr to Max Magee, or from Terry Bradshaw to Lynn Swann. No, the most memorable throw in Super Bowl history didn't come from the arm of Roger Staubach, Joe Namath, Steve Young, Doug Williams, or Troy Aikman. Rather, it weakly slipped from the palm of an Armenian soccer player named Garo Yepremian.

The diminutive, balding Yepremian looked more like a baker than a football player. He had been a soccer star in Cyprus before coming to America to gain fame as the place-kicker for the Miami Dolphins. He became famous for uttering the phrase, "I keek a touchdown!" about his NFL job, but became infamous for the only pass attempt of his NFL career.

With the Dolphins playing the Washington Redskins in Super Bowl VII, Yepremian took center stage in America's biggest sporting event. The game was played before more than 90,000 spectators at the Los Angeles Coliseum, with millions more watching by television around the world.

Miami led the Redskins 14-0 in the fourth quarter as Yepremian trotted onto the field to attempt a 42-yard field goal. The Dolphins were enjoying a perfect season, undefeated in 16 games. And a successful kick at this point in the game could secure the game for Miami — and ensure the only perfect season ever for an NFL team. It was then that Yepremian created one of the most memorable blunders in sports history.

The soccer-style field-goal attempt left Yepremian's foot with a low trajectory. Low enough for the Redskins front line to block the kick, and send the ball back toward the kicker. The ball bounced into Yepremian's hands. The startled kicker had never had the ball in his hands for a play before, so when it happened here, he appeared as though he was holding a ticking bomb.

Instead of falling on the ball, the panicked kicker began to scramble away from the mass of bodies at the line of scrimmage, looking for someone to whom he could throw the ball.

It is important to note here that Yepremian had never thrown a football in a real game before. In fact, the first football game he kicked in was also the first game he had ever seen. Nonetheless, here he was, in the biggest game of his life, with the football in his hands, rolling out and looking for a receiver.

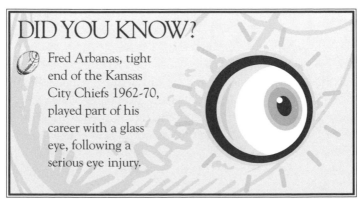

DID YOU KNOW?

Fred Arbanas, tight end of the Kansas City Chiefs 1962-70, played part of his career with a glass eye, following a serious eye injury.

"As soon as I picked it (the ball) up, my mind went blank, and I'm not sure exactly what I did," Yepremian would explain after the game.

What he did was attempt a feeble "pass"—to whom, no one is quite sure. In a scene that looked like it came from a Three Stooges film, Yepremian's arm moved forward, but the ball did not. The ball went two feet straight up over the kicker's head. As it came down, Yepremian made a volleyball-like swipe at it, but missed. Unfortunately, the ball settled into the waiting arms of Redskins defensive back Mike Bass. With nothing but green and a 5'6", 135-pound kicker in front of him, Bass took off for the end zone.

Yepremian, who had also never made a tackle in his football career, swiped at Bass and missed in that attempt as well. Forty-nine yards later, the Redskins had a touchdown that cut the lead to 14-7 and put Miami's perfect season in serious jeopardy—and Yepremian had created one of the most-replayed sports highlights ever.

"I never prayed so much before," said Yepremian of the game's waning moments, as he watched his teammates hold on for 14-7 victory and protect their undefeated record. In the end, the moment was good for a laugh, which it has continued to evoke with countless replays over thirty years. Still, for Garo Yepremian, the moment was anything but humorous.

"I feel so very bad," he told the awaiting media after the game. "The only time I ever throw the ball is in practice when I throw to the guys just for fun. This wasn't fun."

ALL-OUTDOORS TEAM:

WALT ROCK	EMLEN TUNNELL
CHARLIE WATERS	RONNIE LOTT
RON EAST	RANDY MOSS
ED WEST	BOB LILLY
WILLIE WOOD	CHIP BANKS
WARREN SAPP	PAT BEACH
HOWARD MUDD	CLIFF BRANCH
RYAN LEAF	CRAIG COTTON
JACK SNOW	MIKE CURRENT
KEN STONE	JIMMY ORR
ED STORM	STEVE AUGUST
CARNELL LAKE	RAY MAY
LARRY POOLE	LEROY KEYES
BOBBY MAPLES	DERRICK HATCHETT

A GIANT ERROR

Next to Garo Yepremian's attempted Super Bowl pass, perhaps the most infamous bonehead play in the NFL occurred in 1978, when the New York Giants took on the Philadelphia Eagles at the Meadowlands in New Jersey. One of Yepremian's teammates from the 1973 Super Bowl Dolphins played a key role in this situation as well.

Larry Csonka, Super Bowl MVP for Miami, was finishing his career as the fullback of the hapless Giants. New York held a rare lead over the Eagles, by the score of 17-12, late in the game. The Giants had the ball on their own 29 yard line with just 31 seconds left to play. The Eagles were out of timeouts. All New York quarterback Joe Pisarcik had to do was take the snap from center one more time and fall on the ball. Then the clock would run out without another play and the Giants would win.

But rather than calling for such a play, New York offensive coordinator Bob Gibson inexplicably called for a running play, with Pisarcik handing off to Csonka. The play entailed greater risk, as the ball had to exchange hands twice, which meant the chance of a fumble increased. Still, the play was called, and the players attempted to execute it.

It was doomed from the beginning. Pisarcik didn't have a good grip on the ball as he stumbled away from the center. As he turned to put the ball into Csonka's belly, he collided with the stocky running back, and the ball dropped to the turf—as the quarterback and fullback knocked each other down. The ball bounced right to alert Eagles defensive back Herman Edwards, who scooped it up and ran untouched into the end zone.

The Giants lost 19-17. The next day, Bob Gibson was fired.

DID YOU KNOW?

Two current NFL teams were named after real people – one for a football man, the other for a historical figure. They are the Cleveland Browns, for Paul Brown, and the Buffalo Bills, for "Buffalo Bill" Cody.

ALL-GEOGRAPHY TEAM:

KEITH LINCOLN

KEN HOUSTON

JOE MONTANA

WARREN MOON

DOUG FRANCE

TOM LONDON

BUBBA PARIS

YALE LARY

RUSSELL MARYLAND

ROBERT BRAZILE

JERRY RHOME

DAVID BOSTON

MARYLAND

GET ME TO THE GAME ON TIME

On August 19, 1982, the Atlanta Braves called up rookie pitcher Pascual Perez from the minor leagues. The animated, rail-thin Dominican became a legend in Atlanta that day, the day he was to make his Major League debut for the Braves in a start against the Montreal Expos.

Perez, a 25-year-old who spoke little English, had qualified for his Georgia driver's license earlier in the day and believed himself capable of driving to the ballpark. However, as he tried to navigate his way around the Atlanta area, he got lost. So he drove around, and around, and around.

Three times he circled Atlanta on Interstate 285, the highway that loops the metropolitan Atlanta area. Each time he missed the exit for the stadium. He drove for so long that at one point he ran out of gas. Realizing he had no money, he borrowed ten dollars from a gas station attendant

to pay for enough fuel to make it to the stadium, which he finally did—during the game's second inning.

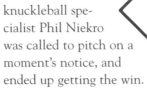

Meanwhile, durable Braves knuckleball specialist Phil Niekro was called to pitch on a moment's notice, and ended up getting the win.

The following night, Perez made it to the park on time and pitched into the 10th inning of a 2-1, extra-innings victory.

Perez's teammates took the incident in stride, but they did take action, in a good-natured effort to remind the pitcher of his blunder. A few days later, Braves players presented Perez with a brand new warm-up jacket—with the number I-285 emblazoned on the back.

WORDS TO LIVE BY

"Love never fails, character never quits,

and with patience and persistence,

dreams do come true."

PETE MARAVICH

member of the NBA's 50th Anniversary All-Time Team

BAD HAIR DAY

I n 1983, Utah Jazz guard Jerry Eaves was killing time on the road prior to a big game against the Phoenix Suns. Eaves found a local Phoenix shop in which to get his hair cut. Unfortunately for Eaves, it was a bad day for the salon. He was quite disappointed, and somewhat embarrassed when he saw the results. A large bald spot was apparent atop his head, courtesy of a careless barber. Distraught, Eaves gathered a clump of hair that had been cut from his head, took it with him, and used an adhesive to attach it to the bald spot.

During the game that evening, as Eaves was running down the court, the clump of hair fell out and landed on the court. Eaves reached down, grabbed the hair and stuffed it in his pants. Eaves then took himself out of the game and headed for the locker room, where he borrowed a car from the team's director of broadcasting, Dave Fredman, and drove back to the team hotel, where he glued the hair clump back into place over the bald spot. Once the hair was back in place, Eaves returned to the arena.

This time, the hair clump stayed in place, but by game's end, Eaves had acquired a new nickname that also stuck. Team broadcaster Rod Hundley immediately began calling Eaves "Razor," which became his new moniker around the league.

ALL ROYALTY TEAM:

G- TAYSHAUN PRINCE

G- BILLY KNIGHT

C- SEAN ROOKS

F- BERNARD KING

F- DONALD ROYAL

ALL PARLIAMENTARY TEAM:

G- GAIL BISHOP

G- BRIAN CARDINAL

C- BOB RULE

F- WALTER DUKES

F- ACIE EARL

ALL WALL STREET TEAM:

G- PHIL BOND

G- MARK PRICE

C- LARON PROFIT

F- ERIC MONEY

F- GENE BANKS

ONE ON FIVE

In 1972, the West Coast Christian College Knights were taking on the University of California at Santa Cruz in a basketball game, when they found themselves in serious foul trouble.

With just over two minutes left in the game, the Knights led the Sea Lions of Santa Cruz by the score of 70-57. But that seemingly comfortable lead was in serious jeopardy.

Every player on the WCCC team had fouled out, with the exception of guard Mike Lockhart, and he had four fouls—one away from disqualification.

"We started the game in a tandem zone," Lockhart explained after the game, "then we went to a straight two-three zone. After we were down to four guys we used a two-two box. Then with three players—a one-two diamond. Then—with two players —a one-one zone. Finally a one."

Incredibly, Lockhart was only outscored 10-5 by the five Santa Cruz players during the game's final two minutes, and he single-handedly held on to secure the Knights a 75-67 victory.

IF AT FIRST YOU DON'T SUCCEED

While attempting to qualify for the 1960 Portland (Oregon) City Amateur Golf Championship, Kelley Stroud amazed onlookers with his display of ineptitude and mastery.

On the par-three 16th hole, Stroud hit his tee shot into the water hazard. His second attempt from the tee also splashed down into the water, as did his third. As he lined up for his fourth attempt, Stroud had already accumulated 6 shots (including three penalty strokes)

and was yet to put a ball in play.

However, on his fourth swing, Stroud hit his ball 148 yards straight into the cup, giving him an amazing four-over-par hole in one.

EXTREME JUMPING

During a 1959 skiing tournament in Duluth, Minnesota, 26-year-old Chuck Ryan lined up at the top of the ski jump ramp for his first attempt. He glided down the jump, hit the bottom of the ramp and launched himself into the air with good form. However, he had one small problem. Upon thrusting himself into the air at the takeoff point, Ryan somehow managed to jump out of his skis. His bindings came loose, and his skis were left at the bottom of the jump as Ryan flew into the air.

With a startled crowd looking on, Ryan soared 150 feet without his skis, but managed to land without harm. He later said it was his quick thinking that saved him from injury, as he adjusted his body so he could, "come sliding in like a ballplayer into second base."

Shaken but unhurt, Ryan was eager to get back up the hill and jump again.

WRONG ARM

Tommy John was one of the most successful pitchers of the 1970s and '80s. For the Chicago White Sox, Los Angeles Dodgers, New York Yankees, and California Angels, the lefthander won 286 games over 25 seasons, was a four-time all-star, and pitched in three World Series.

But to many baseball fans, John is best known for the groundbreaking arm surgery he underwent in 1974. Doctor Frank Jobe pioneered a successful ligament transplant surgery on John, allowing the pitcher to come back and pitch for nearly two more decades. The innovative operation gave hope to pitchers who suffered arm injuries that before were career-ending. So linked was John to the surgical procedure, that in being prescribed for other pitchers, it henceforth became known throughout baseball circles as Tommy John Surgery.

While the operation did revive John's career, it did take some of the steam off his once-potent fastball. He was forced to become craftier, to pitch to more pinpoint locations, and to change speeds more often. He did so and became a consistent winner.

Through it all, he kept a sense of humor about his experience. In speaking to the press about the less-intimidating fastball after his comeback, John talked of the pitcher he most admired, the legendary Sandy Koufax.

John told the media that prior to his surgery, he jokingly told his doctors to "put in a Koufax fastball."

"And, they did," he said. "But it was Mrs. Koufax's!"

SEND ONE TO THE MOON

Pitcher Gaylord Perry was a master of making hitters look foolish. Throughout a Major League career that spanned 20 seasons, Perry earned Cy Young Awards in both the National and American leagues and won more than 300 games. He was an all-star who played for the San Francisco Giants, Cleveland Indians, San Diego Padres, and New York Yankees.

He is best remembered for how deeply he frustrated hitters. Nearly everyone of his era knew Perry used an illegal substance on the ball to throw a "spitball," but no one could prove it. Perry was checked by umpires numerous times throughout his career, but was never caught with the goods. Knowing that his reputation as a spitballer gave him a mental advantage over hitters, Perry toyed with his opponents.

Before every pitch he entered into a routine of touching his fingers to the bill of his cap, wiping them across the hair behind his ears, and touching them to various parts of his uniform—all spots where Vaseline or some other substance could be concealed. His routine drove hitters crazy.

Often, upon striking out on a pitch that moved like a spitter, opposing batters would yell at Perry as they angrily stomped back to the dugout.

For all of Perry's success on the mound, he hardly made a mark at the plate, becoming one of the weakest-hitting pitchers of his era. In 1963, as a rookie for the San Francisco Giants, Perry jokingly told the press of his hitting, "They'll put a man on the moon before I hit a home run."

Amazingly, on July 20, 1969, just a few hours after Neil Armstrong became the first man to set foot on the moon, Gaylord Perry hit the first home run of his career.

In 1983, Perry retired with 314 career pitching victories, placing him in the top 20 in baseball history. He also finished with only one lifetime home run.

ALL-CULINARY TEAM:

JOHNNY SAMPLE

DWIGHT SCALES

ROOSEVELT LEAKS

MIKE LEMON

DENNIS LICK

BEN COATES

JERRY RICE

BART OATES

DAVE PEAR

BUBBA BEAN

MILT PLUM

REGGIE TONGUE

LOUIS LIPPS

JACK HAM

CHRIS HANBURGER

COY BACON

TOM BEER

JARVIS REDWINE

DERON CHERRY

JUNIOR COFFEY

BILL CURRY

DAN BUNZ

GOOD ANSWER?

S teve Spurrier is known as one of the most innovative coaches in all of football. He has won at every level and has fashioned some of the most prolific offensives the game has ever seen. One of the keys to his success is that he is a perfectionist who demands much from his players.

Perhaps that mindset comes as a result of his experiences as an NFL player in the 1970s. Spurrier was the quarterback for the hapless 1976 Tampa Bay Buccaneers, who became the only team in NFL history to lose every game of the regular season, finishing at 0-16.

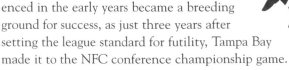

The futility the Bucs experi-enced in the early years became a breeding ground for success, as just three years after setting the league standard for futility, Tampa Bay made it to the NFC conference championship game.

Still, several Bucs plays from '76 have made the various "blooper reels" sports fans see for sale on TV. Dropped passes, fumbles, missed tackles, and kicks that went awry—the Bucs were a comedy of errors, both on the field and in the locker room. The coach of the Bucs was noted quipster John McKay, who had won college national championships at USC before taking the job in Tampa. McKay's one-liners were well-documented by the beat writers who covered the '76 team and are still fondly remembered. They also made an impact on Bucs' players such as Spurrier.

"I remember a speech McKay was giving us at one point in the season," Spurrier recalls. "He was emphasizing that games were lost in the trenches by failing to block and tackle on the front lines.

"And as he was talking he noticed a lineman asleep in the back. He called his name, woke him up, and asked, 'Where are most games lost?' And the lineman says, 'Right here in Tampa, sir.'"

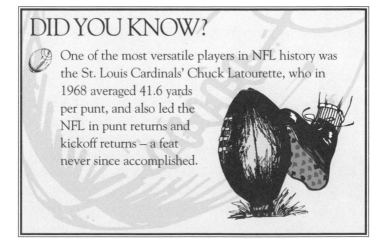

DID YOU KNOW?

One of the most versatile players in NFL history was the St. Louis Cardinals' Chuck Latourette, who in 1968 averaged 41.6 yards per punt, and also led the NFL in punt returns and kickoff returns – a feat never since accomplished.

HORSE OR BRONKO?

B ronko Nagurski was one of the greatest players of the early era of professional football. A college All-American at both running back and defensive lineman, Nagurski was known for his toughness and strength.

During a game against the New York Giants in the 1930s, Nagurski took a hand-off and rambled up the middle toward the end zone. Giants defensive back Benny Friedman hit Nagurski at the 12-yard line but could not bring him down until Nagurski had surged forward another eleven yards.

After the play, Friedman turned to his teammates and coaches on the sideline and said of Nagurski, "He hits hard enough to knock down a horse."

Incredibly, on the next play, Nagurski was given the ball again, and did just as Friedman said. He barreled his way through the Giants defense, into the end zone for a touchdown. In his determination to score, Nagurski worked up such a head of steam that after he bashed his way through the defenders, his momentum carried him into a mounted policeman stationed at the back of the end zone. Nagurski crashed into the horse and rider and knocked them both to the ground.

Not realizing what he had run into, Nagurski jumped up to his feet and somewhat confused declared, "That last man hit me awful hard!"

Shortly after this incident, in an effort to protect both animals and humans from the powerful Nagurski, football's residing powers determined that end zones would have to be lengthened.

ALL-VOCATION TEAM:

TED PROVOST

KING HILL

JEFF QUEEN

DAVID KNIGHT

LAWYER MILLOY

GERALD TINKER

ALAN PAGE

SAM BAKER

MIKE BARBER

GLENN RESSLER

BOB JURY

GREG COOK

TOM TONER

TOMMY MASON

DENNIS LAW

IRVING FRYAR

SECOND CAREERS:

These NFL stars had prominent second careers after their playing days ended:

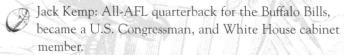

Jack Kemp: All-AFL quarterback for the Buffalo Bills, became a U.S. Congressman, and White House cabinet member.

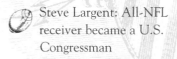

Steve Largent: All-NFL receiver became a U.S. Congressman

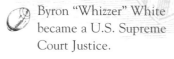

Byron "Whizzer" White became a U.S. Supreme Court Justice.

Fred Dryer, former L.A. Rams
defensive end,
became an actor.

 Actor Paul Robeson was
one of the NFL's early
stars before turning to
the stage

 Running back Herman
Wedemeyer was a regular
on the television series
Hawaii Five-O.

 Hall of Fame defensive tackle
Merlin Olsen was a regular on the
television series *Little House on the Prairie*.

 Grammy Award winning songwriter Mike Reid once
played defensive tackle for the Cincinnati Bengals.

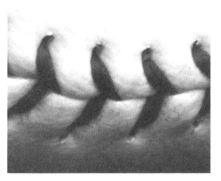

 Bo Jackson, Deion
Sanders, Brian
Jordan, Chad
Hutchinson, and
Tom Brown all
played in both the
NFL and Major
League Baseball.

EXTREME TEAMWORK

Former baseball slugger Albert Belle was one of the game's most-feared power hitters during the 1990s. He hit more than 300 home runs in a career cut short by injuries. In 1995 he belted 50 long balls, putting him in elite company at that point in the game's history. But teammates and opponents alike all had a feeling that Belle used cork to illegally doctor his bats, in an effort to make the ball travel farther. In fact, it was said of Belle that he used enough cork to put a couple of vineyards out of business.

In 1994, Belle was caught in a caper that made Major League baseball look like a sequel to *Mission Impossible*. Midway into the season, Belle's Cleveland Indians faced the Chicago White Sox in Cleveland.

Following one of Belle's trips to the plate, Sox manager Gene Lamont approached the umpiring crew to voice his suspicion that Belle's bats were corked. Crew chief Dave Phillips also had seen and heard enough to make him question whether or not Belle was playing according to the rules. So he confiscated the bat that Belle used in that game and had the bat placed in his locker in the umpires' dressing room. He was to have the bat X-rayed following the game to determine whether or not it was corked.

The Indians knew Belle was headed for trouble, as they knew the bat was corked. So, they set out to replace the bat that was put in Phillips's locker.

While the game continued, Indians pitcher Jason Grimsley went into the clubhouse. He wriggled through a crawl space that led him to a spot in the ceiling just above the umpires' locker room. Then he dropped through an escape hatch, opened up Phillips's locker, removed the corked bat, and replaced it with a legal one.

"My heart was going a thousand miles a second," Grimsley later said of his cat burglar-like escapade. "I just rolled the dice."

The dice didn't come up a winner for Grimsley.

You see, each batter has a selection of bats with his own name on the label. In his rush to switch the bats, Grimsley put a replacement bat in Phillips's locker, one with teammate Paul Sorrento's name on it. It didn't take long for Phillips to figure out what had happened. Once matters were all sorted out, Belle was suspended for seven games.

Later, in his autobiography, Indians shortstop Omar Vizquel said of the memorable event, "I can be naive at times, but I'm not stupid. Certainly not stupid enough to steal Albert's corked bat and replace it with one that looked completely different—one that was autographed by Paul Sorrento. That wasn't even a nice try."

Then Vizquel added, "The problem, of course, was that all of Albert's bats were corked."

ALL FIELD & STREAM TEAM:

G- DOC RIVERS

G- KENDALL GILL

C- MATT FISH

F- MICHAEL BROOKS

F- DEWAYNE SCALES

ALL OUTDOORS TEAM:

G- GENE ROCK

G- PERRY MOSS

C- CHEROKEE PARKS

F- ADRIAN BRANCH

F- GENE STUMP

SPACE JAM

Shawn Marion made an immediate impact on the Phoenix Suns during his rookie season in 1999. He proved to be a big-time scorer who could shoot from the outside and also take the ball inside among the big men.

In a memorable game against the Houston Rockets in December of his rookie season, Marion was in for a Christmas surprise. After a jump ball, he scooped the ball up off the floor, sprinted toward the hoop uncontested, and went up for what was to be a thundering slam-dunk. But while he was in mid-air, Marion suddenly realized there was a reason he had been uncontested on his way to the basket—he was about to jam the ball in the wrong hoop. Rockets' players looked on in delight as they waited for the gift two-pointer.

But Marion quickly made a split-second adjustment while he hung in the air and in desperation tried to fling the ball back to a teammate. As soon as he did this, he was whistled for a backcourt violation.

Marion tried to laugh the whole thing off, but his teammates were not about to let him forget his mistake. They quickly dubbed him, Shawn "Wrong Way" Marion.

ALL WRITERS ARE ALIKE

The lovable Yogi Berra is one of the most endearing athletes in all of sport. His words have been quoted around the world by people of all cultures. But Berra himself was not much of a reader. In fact, during his playing days he used to tell people that the only thing he read was the sports page.

Once, at a restaurant in New York following a game, Berra was introduced to Ernest Hemingway. After the meeting, someone asked Berra if he had ever read anything that the famous writer had written.

"I don't think so," Berra replied. "What paper does he write for?"

(Ironically, Hemingway, before achieving literary fame, wrote for the *Toronto Star*.)

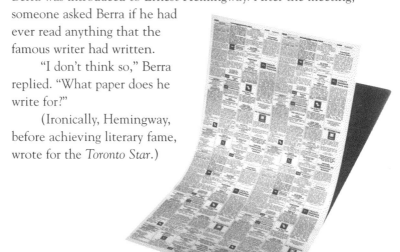

GENTLY DOWN THE STREAM

The Olympic games have long been a display of sportsmanship and human drama, even above winning. Perhaps at no time was that more evident than during the 1928 summer games, in the rowing competition.

Among the competitors participating in the single-scull event was Australian Henry Pearce, who was a true gentleman.

Pearce was leading the race when a family of ducks suddenly passed before him in single file across the water.

Undaunted, Pearce courteously raised his oars out of the water and waited for the downy family to pass. Then he resumed rowing, all the way to a gold-medal finish.

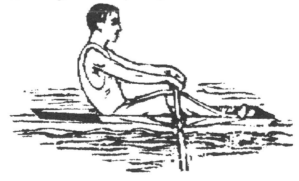

GRIMM OUTLOOK

Charlie Grimm was a well-respected manager for thirteen years for the Chicago Cubs during baseball's golden era in the 1930s and '40s. He led the Cubs to three World Series and was known as a no-nonsense leader who always said exactly what he was thinking.

One day, Grimm received a call from a Cub's scout. "Charlie!" the scout cried with excitement, "I've landed the greatest young pitcher in the land! He struck out every man who came to bat—twenty-seven in a row. Nobody even got a foul off him until two were out in the ninth. The pitcher is right here with me. What shall I do?"

"Sign up the guy who got the foul," Grimm replied. "We're looking for hitters."

TOO BIG

Marty Springstead, longtime supervisor and executive director of American League umpires, said he will never forget his first assignment as a Major League ump, calling balls and strikes behind the plate.

The year was 1966, and Springstead was calling a game involving the Washington Senators at JFK stadium in Washington DC.

Bunyan-esque slugger Frank Howard was a star for the Senators at the time, and at 6-7 and 250 pounds, he was the game's largest specimen, and one of the most fearsome men to step to the plate in all of baseball.

On the first pitch to the mountainous power hitter, Springstead called a knee-high fastball a strike.

Howard turned around and yelled at the rookie umpire: "Get something straight, buster! I don't know where you came from or how you got to the Major Leagues, but don't call that pitch on me a strike. Understand?"

The next pitch was in the same spot, and Springstead yelled, "Two!"

"Two what?" Howard bellowed.

"Too low," Springstead said. "Much too low."

DON'T UNPACK YOUR BAGS

The legendary Casey Stengel had many great seasons managing the New York Yankees. He led the Bronx Bombers to seven World Series championships in his 12 seasons with the team.

Over his 25 years as a manager, Stengel's name became almost synonymous with success, as he won 1,926 games. But when he took over as the skipper of the cross-town New York Mets in 1962, Stengel saw more bad baseball in a year than he had seen in all his days wearing Yankee pinstripes.

Of his team's escapades, Stengel once said, "There comes a time in every man's life at least once, and I've had plenty of them."

One day, shortly after assuming the helm of the Mets, Stengel was asked by New York media about the potential of two of his team's most highly touted prospects, both 20-year-olds making their first attempts at a Major League roster spot.

"In ten years, Ed Kranepool has a chance to be a star," Stengel replied. "And in ten years the other guy has a chance to be thirty."

If you have enjoyed this book,
Hallmark would love
to hear from you.

Please send comments to

Book Feedback
2501 McGee, Mail Drop 250
Kansas City, MO 64141-6580

Or e-mail us at

booknotes@hallmark.com